God's Word:

From My Heart...
to Yours.

Modern Analogies
Illustrating Timeless Scriptures

Alan G. Vandewater

Acknowledgments

My sincere appreciation to all who
inspired me to put this collection
together for the common good.

To all who supported me in my training
and my early efforts: my family, my
mentors, those who critiqued me
and those who added suggestions.

Many thanks to my congregation,
pastors, friends and doctors who
encouraged me; and of course,
to God above who controls all things.

My special thanks to:

The Rev. Bruce Goettsche
The Rev. William Barrett
Evelyn Moyer
Jeff and Doris Roberts
Lisa Sells
Don McIntosh

Why I wrote this book:

Isaiah 61:1,2

> The spirit of the Lord God is upon me,
> because the Lord has anointed me;
> He has sent me to bring good news to the oppressed,
> to bind up the brokenhearted,
> to proclaim liberty to the captives,
> and release to the prisoners;
> to proclaim the year of the Lord's favor.

Romans 8:28

> We know that all things work together for good for those
> who love God, who are called according to His purpose.

Words of Encouragement

Psalm 31:9-13

> Be gracious to me, O Lord, for I am in distress;
> my eye wastes away from grief, my soul and body also.
> For my life is spent in sorrow, and my years with sighing;
> my strength fails, because of my misery, and my bones
> waste away.
> I am the scorn of all my adversaries, a horror to my
> neighbors,
> an object of dread to my acquaintances;
> those who see me in the street flee from me.
> I have passed out of mind like one who is dead;
> I have become like a broken vessel;
> For I hear the whispering of many.

VI

Table of Contents:

VIII

PART ONE

(The Beginning Years)

Pages 11-71

"The Power of Prayer" (A Tribute to My Mom)

Having just spent the entire Thanksgiving week in the hospital, I couldn't help but think of a similar occurrence involving my mother...almost sixteen years before.

Nineteen years ago, while at my sister's for Thanksgiving, Mom got sick and ended up in the hospital in grave condition. My family prudently decided not to notify me until danger had passed, but they did eventually notify me as to what had transpired.

It seems that Mom could have been very near death. She somehow managed to stall that ominous fate by hook or crook, or perhaps even by a promise to the Higher Power.

Fast forward, three years later. One of my sisters called and said they were planning a surprise birthday party for Mom and would I be able to come. Even though it was short notice, things fell into place. Vacation time remained, airfares were cheap, brothers were coming in from Maine and Massachusetts, I, of course, was coming in from Ohio.

The day of the party, all of us – nieces, nephews, sons and daughters – were preparing a breakfast brunch fit for a queen! What a spread! Mom came up the walk with a sister in tow, while all us boys hid on the cellar steps, the same ones we had traversed as kids at various ages.

This was where things turned weird. Mom was used to the girls being around and popping in, but wasn't prepared to see any boys. First, the youngest, came up the stairs and into the room. No big surprise there. Massachusetts wasn't so far away that an inopportune visit wouldn't be out of the question.

Mom smiled!

Then the middle brother was announced and up he came, startling my Mom even more; this was getting freaky. Maine was a looong way away. But regardless she was glad to see him! So much family in so little space. It was wonderful!

Then it was my turn. I can still see the overwhelming, perplexed look on her face when I came around the corner and approached the room. It was a mixture of surprise, awe, and unfathomable disbelief. All of her sons in one room, together; especially the one whom she only saw one or two days a year – her oldest and firstborn.

Things turned festive and we had a really nice morning. Later on, it was revealed that we had rented out a party room at a nearby restaurant – just for us and in honor of Mom's birthday, her seventy-first. It was almost like the wedding she never had, I thought, as I sat next to her, while she scolded me for wanting to have a taste of her meal.

Soon the weekend was over, and it was time for everyone to leave and head back to their homes and adopted states, to prepare for Christmas. That last evening, after everyone else had left and things were quiet, Mom came up close to me, looked up at her once premature son, and said the most ominous words, which were: "The next time you see me will be at the funeral home." I replied, as I held her tight (for the last time), "Oh Mom…you're not going anywhere." On the way to the airport the next day, I had this overwhelming urge to see Mom once again, but time was short and we didn't want to miss my flight.

Back home, two weeks later, on a chilly Christmas morning; I had just returned from walking our dogs, when I sensed something wasn't right. Everyone was clustered in my daughter's room, in various stages of dress. They told me over hushed tones, that Mom had passed away that very morning around two am; peacefully in her sleep, with her favorite cat curled up beside her.

Another hastily arranged trip home, except this one wouldn't be about celebrating. I thought about how lonely she must've been when I left her standing; weeping at the curb, when I departed Long Island for Ohio with my family, seeking a new beginning.

I thought of how terribly lonesome she must've been after I left on that last night, with her ominous words echoing in my ears.

Then a pattern emerged and I understood completely. She had known ahead of time what was going to happen. She had wanted to see her whole family together again, especially her oldest. This all evolved when plans came together so perfectly for her birthday party.

This was God's plan: between Himself and my Mom. We can only speculate as to what was prayed, what was said, what was promised when she teetered between life and death, that Thanksgiving Eve, three years before. Was it her literal dying wish, to see all her family together just one more time?

I believe there was something in motion here. God does HIS will and I believe somehow, he did it then. How things fell into place so smoothly. Mom even said, that when my sister sets her mind to something, she gets it done (with a little help from above). The cheap airfares, the time available, the freaky way everyone was able to make it. God will wait, but not for long.

I know positively that Mom put on a happy face when I, the oldest appeared in the room; but there was something wrong with the forced smile. There was an important element taking place that she realized, and she wasn't about to let anyone know different. I believe, at that moment, she recalled the transaction that had been made. Her last wish to see us all was taking place and now God was setting things in motion.

To be able to tell me with certainty, that next night, when I saw her and held her, that it would be the last time, must've broken her heart. It was the same way I broke hers, when I left so many years before. Even though I wasn't believing; she knew.

Fourteen days later…it was a done deal. Those last words I ever heard from my Mom were to be my last memory of her. Oh, how I wish I had followed my gut instincts and seen her that next day, one last time, and told her how much I loved her. It reminded me starkly that we know not when the Lord will come to take us home. Mom was in the process of writing "Thank Yous" to us all when it was time. Mine was given to me later; it never made it to the mailbox. God knew it was time.

Christmas Day will forever be a day of sad thoughts lurking with a twinge of guilt. Was I the perfect son? No, I wasn't. But such is the life and understanding between a mother and her precious child – the first-born, the preemie, who in that day and age probably shouldn't have made it. He then grows into her oldest and very last confidante. A pair who had bonded over all that growing up entails. A sharing bond that had weathered so much together. Now those struggles were over. Mom was where Jesus promised and is free from pain, sadness, and heartache.

We know not when the Father will come calling. He has our dwelling place already prepared for us. When it is our time, according to God, he will call us home.

Thanks be to God!

Alan Vandewater
December 1, 2016

"Everything Needful Has Been"

There have been times past when we've gotten really serious talking about our wants vs our needs. For example, our wants go into overtime when we feel the need to resort to stealing in order to satisfy our wants.

One common underlying theme for every commandment is man's desire to change something or do something to satisfy his wants vs his needs. "Honor thy father and thy mother;" "Thou shall not kill;" "Thou shall not steal;" "Thou shall not commit adultery;" "Thou shall not bear false witness;" "Thou shall not covet." Everything we do seems to be based on what we want; rather than what we need! We don't even attempt to recognize what God could do for us; it's always us first! Remember:

"Everything needful has been."

The Israelites, (as pointed out in The Old Testament in Exodus) are lamenting that they should've died by the hand of the Lord, in Egypt, even though they were slaves, because they were happy then. They were happy, simply because they sat by their pots and bowls and had their share of breads and meats until they were full. They were never hungry! They didn't have to worry about where their next meal was coming from. But now in the wilderness, where they were free, they were not sure if they would survive. God heard their laments and just to remind them that He was still there, graciously supplied them with the needed bread and meat. The people needed to be reminded that

"Everything needful has been."

So, getting back to ourselves and our wants. Are we like the Israelites in that we forget that everything we need for our very existence comes from God? Our daily bread comes in the form of all things necessary for daily life: food, clothing, all the elements needed to make them possible; land, fields, sunshine, the earth, and all that is in it. Oceans, homes and property. Work and income. A good government that protects us as best as possible, from anything that would keep us from fully enjoying God's gifts. We have science and technology and the machinery to make our lives fruitful. We generally have peace and health, we have a good name, good friends and good neighbors.

"Everything needful has been."

Even though God provides us with our needs, especially if we pray for them, we also ask Him for more: protection from the work of the Devil: calamities, war, pestilence, fire, floods, and all the things that will keep us from having faith in our God and the things He has given us. It seems these things only come when we waver and drift away from God.

So where do we draw the line between our wants and needs? Is having too many wants a bad thing? Are our wants going to be taken away from us, as can be the case with stealing? Are we going to lose our excesses in one way or another, so that we can't enjoy them? Are we violating God's gifts by being greedy, selfish, hoarding things, or obtaining things to appease our own wants? This only gives the Devil more opportunities to make us disregard what God has in mind for us. Remember, God will take care of us.

"Everything needful has been."

We've all heard the phrase; "You can't take it with you." Come to think of it, I've never once seen a U-Haul truck in a funeral procession, dutifully taking someone's possessions to their new home. We are here on Earth, along with all our earthly possessions, simply because of God's grace. Without His hand we do not exist!

Without His grace we have nothing! In my own life, I may not have a mansion; but I do have a warm and secure home. I may not have filet-mignon every night; but I don't go to bed hungry either. I'm not thrilled about my job; but at least I have one. My family loves me, in spite of my faults. I still have most of my health, and I'm able to use my time and talents to do such things as preaching to you. This is all God's doing...not ours!

"Everything needful has been."

Maybe we're looking for the wrong "daily bread." Maybe we're too concerned about "keeping our bellies full" with the wrong things! This is not to say the things we've talked about are wrong; they are all God's gifts. At the end of our first reading today Moses replies: "It is the bread that the Lord has given you to eat." This is prophetic, especially when we get to the Gospel. Up until now the people following Jesus had never seen anyone more important than Moses. Jesus now tells them not to work for food that will perish, but for the food that endures for eternal life.

The Israelites expound on the fact that their ancestors ate manna, which was a gift from Heaven. Jesus says: "It was not Moses who gave you the bread from Heaven; but my Father who gives you the true bread, from Heaven." "For the bread of God is that which comes down from Heaven and gives Life to the world." "I am the bread of Life." "Whomever comes to me will never be hungry." Have you not seen?

"Everything needful has been,"
sent by his graceful ordaining!

Thanks be to God!

Alan Vandewater
August 13, 2000

2 Peter 1: vs 3

3 His divine power has given us everything needed for life and for god-
liness, through the knowledge of him who called us by his own glory
and goodness.

"How Good, Lord, to Be Here" ("Fishers of Men")

How good, Lord, to be here! We could've made other choices this morning, such as: sleeping in, doing laundry, doing odd jobs or whatever. Instead we made a choice to be here in the company of our fellow Christians; to be able to greet our brothers and sisters with exuberance and excitement, because we have heard the good news and what it means for us! Somewhere back in time...someone made a choice for us, as did the ones before them and the ones before them, and so on; that a certain someone would influence us and include us so that we would believe, that we would learn of God's grace to us, through His son, Jesus Christ. My certain someone happened to be my Mom. I vividly remember us going through everything: Sunday School, Vacation Bible School, and how we agonized, she and I, as we read and memorized the church's required readings. The end result of all this knowledge and along with God's grace is that we learn that we have an obligation. We are obligated to God, to use our talents and God given gifts, to "make disciples of all nations."

We are fortunate that we live in a society which, for the most part, allows us to worship in peace. To proclaim God's love for us without fear of harassment, torture, or even death. It was not always this way. The early Christians in the beginning of "The Church of Christ" were mocked and slaughtered. St. Stephen was stoned to death for his beliefs, but he never wavered in his faith. St Paul in all his travels as "the least of the Apostles," was imprisoned twice and finally beheaded.

But that was a long ago, ancient history, we say, and things are different now. Are they really? It has never been easy for us Christians, and the fight is far from over. All through the ages and even right now we Christians battle oppressors who refuse to believe that Jesus died for our salvation. Do we have the strength and the faith to battle the war that continues for us, even as we speak?

When did this battle begin? In all actuality it began at the Creation. The Bible says: "In the beginning was the Word, and the Word was with God; and the Word was God." In our realm of things, we generally consider the time of Christ's being here on Earth as the beginning of the early church. Jesus, as we are told in the Gospels, is in the process of forming his early church, here on Earth, even though the "Word" was with God from the very beginning of time.

Luke's Gospel Chapter 5 verses 1-11 we find that the crowds are pushing in on Jesus so He retreats into a boat and moves out onto the water just far enough away that the crowds can't reach him. Jesus then proceeds to teach the people from the boat. Let's look at this story from another perspective.

Jesus initially puts out into shallow water off the shore. Why? Because being out of the reach of the crowd symbolizes that the shallow water is safe. After Jesus finishes teaching the crowds, he says authoritatively for Simon to put out into the deeper waters for a catch. Simon protests that they've worked all night and have caught nothing; but at this moment he makes a choice. Out of respect for Jesus, Simon does as he is told. But in his own mind he is convinced that nothing will come of this. After all; Jesus may be a good carpenter and a great teacher, but he's certainly not the expert on fishing that Simon Peter is.

It's been said that you can't catch fish in the middle of a hot day! Fish do not like warm water and will retreat to deeper, cooler waters. Fishermen of that day didn't fish the deep waters of the Sea of Galilee, because of its penchant for violent, unpredictable storms. If caught in one, you could lose everything, perhaps even your life, to the swirling seas! Besides, even if they did catch fish, it would take too long and be too much work to be to their advantage. So, for these reasons, the Galileans chose to stay close to shore where it was safe. They fished in the late evenings and early mornings when the water was cool and the fish were closer to shore. They were willing to fish for less, in exchange for being safe. Jesus knows exactly what he is doing when he tells them to go farther out and cast their nets. When the fishermen do drop their nets, anticipating a long futile effort, they are amazed at the rapidity and the sheer quantity of fish they catch against all odds – especially after experiencing a total flop the night before under prime conditions. Simon realizes then, as do all the others, that Jesus is the Lord and that if they have faith, they can accomplish great things through God. Jesus reaffirms their feelings by saying: "Do not be afraid; from now on you will be catching people." The men's faith was strong enough now to cause them to give up everything and follow Him.

Like them, we have choices, but do we have the faith? Let me pass on a true story that happened to me. A long time ago my wife and I decided to move to Ohio for a fresh start and for no other reason, except that we had relatives here. Decision being made, we moved smoothly through the process of moving; selling the house; and getting rid of things not needed in our new home. Like Simon, I was proud of how smoothly things were going under my expert organization.

As we neared our departure date, I thought a call to my new employer was in order, just to make sure things were "all right." Things were not "all right." The bottom had fallen out of the market, my contact said. Because of this it was not prudent for the company to take on any more employees. I told him I understood the situation, and quietly hung up the phone, and stood there in utter shock! I then staggered the few steps to the kitchen doorway where my wife was cooking and just stood there numbly. Seeing the look on my face, she asked tentatively, "What's the matter?" I replied, "They don't have a job for me in Ohio." Growing panicky and looking for a reassuring answer, she asked me, "What are we going to do?" "I don't know," I answered. Here I was with a wife, a three-year old daughter, a one-year old son, no transportation, no job, and in less than a week we would be out on the street.

Then, emerging across from where I was standing, where for thousands of times there was simply a knot in the knotty pine cabinet, there looking directly at me was the face of Jesus. As I tried to register just what I was seeing, I could sense this warm envelope of peace surround me. I could feel this tremendous weight being lifted off my shoulders. At the same time I could hear His voice telling me: "Go; do not worry. I am with you." As His strong words filled me and gave me strength, I stood tall and told my wife, "We're going." "We can't be any worse off there than we are here." All these years I thought that perhaps, like it says in "Footprints in the Sand," Jesus simply carried me over life's rough hurdles. Then it suddenly dawned on me. As with Simon, Jesus knew exactly what he was doing. Jesus was testing me to see if I had the faith and the strength to follow him, to make the right choice.

Would this be my deep water? Did Jesus take me away from the shallow waters, where it was safe? Away from the neighborhood I grew up in; away from friends that I had; away from my family and all that was familiar? Did he test me to see if I would make the right choice, to follow him and seek out the deep waters, because that's where the most fish are? Did he foresee a day when I would be preaching to my fellow men? Did he see a need for me to bring the word of God to those who need it most?

We need to remember that even in the deepest, stormiest waters, we all are one in mission. We all are one in his call. We all have the gifts and talents God gave us, to be "fishers of people." But do we have the strength and faith? God has given us choices. What are they going to be?

Thanks be to God!

Alan Vandewater
February 4, 2001

Luke 5:1-11

1 Once while Jesus was standing by the lake of Gennesaret, and the crowd was pressing in on him to hear the word of God, 2 he saw two boats there at the shore of the lake; the fishermen had gone out of them and were washing their nets. 3 He got into one of the boats, the one belonging to Simon, and asked him to put out a little way from the shore. Then he sat down and taught the crowds from the boat. 4 When he had finished speaking, he said to Simon, "Put out into the deep water and let down your nets for a catch." 5 Simon answered, "Master, we have worked all night long but have caught nothing. Yet if you say so, I will let down the nets." 6 When they had done this, they caught so many fish that their nets were beginning to break. 7 So, they signaled their partners in the other boat to come and help them. And they came and filled both boats, so they began to sink. 8 But when Simon Peter saw it, he fell down at Jesus' knees, saying, "Go away from me, Lord, for I am a sinful man!" 9 For he and all that were with him were amazed at the catch of fish that they had taken; 10 and so also were James and John, sons of Zebedee, who were partners with Simon. Then Jesus said to Simon, "Do not be afraid; from now on you will be catching people." 11 When they had brought their boats to shore, they left everything and followed him.

"Listening to John the Baptist"

Christmas is coming! Yes; it's coming very soon! Things are going to happen that will (or should) bring smiles to our faces. We can look forward to the Christmas trees, the festive decorations, and the anticipated get-togethers. Even Santa Claus will come, checking his list twice, to find out who's been naughty or nice. Gee; it sounds like even Christmas comes with a risk.

In the Gospel, we find that Mark begins his revelation with a title: "The beginning of the Good News, of Jesus Christ, the Son of God." Mark doesn't start his accounts with the birth of Jesus; he begins with the God-inspired promises of the prophets Isaiah and Malachi. Isaiah and Malachi basically say the same thing as noted here from Malachi 3:vs 1.

> "See, I am sending my messenger to
> prepare the way before me, and the Lord
> you seek, will suddenly come to his temple."
> "The messenger of the Covenant in whom you
> delight indeed; he is coming; says the Lord
> of Hosts."

John didn't just appear out of the woodwork. He is simply the fulfillment of the prophecies of Isaiah and Malachi. In those days, kings sent messengers to announce the kings coming and to literally make the commute as easy and as comfortable as possible. John's job was to prepare the way for the king of kings, Jesus Christ. He did this by preaching to the people; to get them to prepare themselves for the Lord's coming. Further emphasizing John as a prophet and messenger, and not someone royal, was his simple attire and his eating habits, which couldn't have been more spartan. John's preaching centered around the coming judgment, the need for repentance, and the coming of the Messiah.

In Matthew 3:5-6 we read:

> "The whole Judean countryside
> and all the people of Jerusalem
> were going out to him, in the River
> Jordan, confessing their sins."

John drew a sharp contrast between his water baptism and Jesus' baptism by the Holy Spirit. John said to the people: "I baptize you with water, but he whose sandals I am not worthy to untie, will baptize you with the Holy Spirit." God spoke to us, in the form of John, a prophet in the wilderness, who proclaimed a baptism of repentance for the forgiveness of sins. This was a kind of warning; a kind of Santa "naughty or nice" deal. Why would we not want to be like John, proclaiming to all the world from the highest mountain, what the Good News is all about?

Sometimes we need to look at things in a different light. Have you ever noticed how we are reading a sentence and suddenly a word will pop out and we'll go back to it, like it was printed in bold print, and realize it looks "funny?" How did we ever come up with such a crazy combination of letters to make this word? Ironically, that word will be on our minds for days! Or how about a rose garden? We've walked past it seeing its beauty many times before, but have we really seen it? You pick one of the flowers and notice for the first time, the intricate folds of the petals, the lifegiving veins contained within them. You notice the stem and the ant crawling up it, its antennae sensing changes in the air. There is a whole new sense of awareness you never noticed before.

We are like this in our lives. All too often we have not fully experienced the past that we inherited but have simply inhabited it. We haven't examined our past in a new way that we've never seen before. We need to see our past in a new light before we can fully understand the future, which we do not yet comprehend. All our lives we've gone through things and events. We pile up tidbits of information and other happenings. If it's not something that we want, then we then adjust and go on our merry way. We adjust; but we don't fundamentally change. We live in our world but haven't seen it for what it really is. We haven't seen it for what God gave us, because we've been too busy doing things "for us" instead of the way it should have been done…God's way.

Sure, every once in a while, we "get enlightened," maybe at New Year's, and we vow to change our ways and drop some bad habits. Perhaps our friends or parents scold us, and we demur to them that we'll change for the better. This would be a start, but it isn't what John had in mind when he wanted us to change. John wanted us to repent; to revise our thinking and confess that we are in bondage to sin and cannot free ourselves. That we cannot go it alone without getting ourselves in trouble. We need to ask ourselves; when was life good? When was it bad? When did it go right and when was it wrong? When was God in charge and when did we try to do it all by ourselves?

We need God's help! A people separated from God by sin, cannot come back to God unless they are summoned; unless God is willing to forgive. God will forgive us through His Son, Jesus Christ, only if we are ready. God is not slow as we think of slow. Peter writes: "He is not slow, and time has no meaning to Him." "He is patient with us; and does not want us to perish; but to come to repentance."

We have been warned again and again that when the judgment comes it will be like a "thief in the night." We will be hastening and desirous of His coming, but will we be ready? Will we be without spot or blemish with our full focus on God? When that bright light appears out of the darkness, like a subway train coming around the bend; and then when its bright headlamp shines on us, will we heed the conductor's call of "All aboard"? Will we be ready?

Will we be able to climb aboard the train to Heaven and salvation without a blemish? Or will we turn our backs and remain mired in our ungrateful lives, because we didn't heed the trainmaster's announcement to repent and "prepare the way?" You are the only one, my friend who can answer that question.

Thanks be to God!

Alan Vandewater
December 8, 2002

Mark 1: vs 1-8

1.The beginning of the good news of Jesus Christ, the Son of God. 2. As it is written in the prophet Isaiah, "See, I am sending my messenger ahead of you, who will prepare your way; 3. the voice of one crying out in the wilderness: Prepare the way of the Lord, make his paths straight," 4. John the Baptizer appeared in the wilderness, proclaiming a baptism of repentance for the forgiveness of sins. 5. And people from the whole Judean countryside and all the people of Jerusalem were going out to him, and were baptized by him in the river Jordan, confessing their sins. 6. Now John was clothed with camel's hair, with a leather belt around his waist, and he ate locusts and wild honey. 7. He proclaimed, "The one who is more powerful than I is coming after me; I am not worthy to stoop down and untie the thong of his sandals. 8. I have baptized you with water; but he will baptize you with the Holy Spirit.

"Hey Mister; Soon There?"

John's vision for us from the book of Revelation reveals to us that something better is in store for us. A "New Jerusalem"; a new Heaven; a new Earth. An expectation that is to us totally unimaginable. An expectation that far exceeds anything we have or know here on Earth. An expectation that is only obtainable to us because of Jesus' death, resurrection and promise.

In spite of this promise, we continue to hold on to the old; focusing our lives on things of this Earth; getting our priorities backwards in the process. We plant our feet here in this world, rather than focusing on the future as we should be. The fact that I had my own priorities backwards was driven home to me by none other than an elderly nursing home resident.

In my younger years I worked for an ambulance company. While we did have emergency runs during my shifts, my primary job was transporting patients from various locations to doctor's offices, hospitals, clinics and so forth. This is how I met Sadie.

Sadie resided in a nursing home where two of my cousins worked. I tried to arrive early so I could chat with them for a few moments and catch up on things as they got Sadie ready to travel. We never got to where we were going on time. Sadie protested every inch of the way. She wouldn't comb her hair; she wouldn't finish her lunch; she wouldn't get dressed. All this, in spite of our pleadings that this was for her own good. Sadie evidently wanted to follow her own agenda. Eventually, after much wrangling, I would get her into my vehicle and we'd be on our way and then it would start! All of a sudden behind me, this gravelly voice would call out…loudly:

"Hey mister; soon there?"

I tried to explain many times to Sadie that we didn't always get to where we wanted to go as quickly as we wanted to. Sometimes things went slowly. Sometimes obstacles got in our way; and sometimes we simply have to wait.

"Oy, Oy, Oy"… complained Sadie

I soon found out that this was Sadie's standard answer to anything she either didn't believe, or something she didn't want to hear. Still she persisted, driven by some unknown force, relentlessly asking me, "Hey mister; soon there?"

One day I had had enough of this, as she started in. Exasperated, I blurted out rudely, "Sadie; Shut up!" "Oy, Oy, Oy" Sadie replied sadly. Even through all this I began to admire this gutsy, tenacious lady. What was driving her? What was she seeking?

Oftentimes, I'd find myself thinking how Sadie might have been in her prime. I could very easily envision her in her well-to-do neighborhood, hosting a party. It wasn't hard to imagine her with her silver-grey hair piled high in a bouffant, a long powder blue gown reaching to the floor, finished off with elegant silver slippers. I imagined her with a champagne glass held upright in her upturned palm, all the while lording over her party guests.

But as time went by those things didn't matter anymore. Present-day concerns like mortgages and taxes were now things of the past. Even how her palliative care costs or funeral expenses were going to be paid for; didn't matter anymore. Sadie wasn't concerned.

In John's Gospel, Chapter 14 Jesus said;

"Do not let your hearts be troubled." "You believe in God, believe also in me."
"In my Father's house; there are many dwelling places." "If it were not so; would I have told you, that I go to prepare a place for you?"
"And if I go to prepare a place for you; I will come again and I will take you unto myself, so that where I am; there you may be also."

Then one day as I arrived at the nursing home to pick Sadie up; I learned that she had passed on about an hour previously. As I paused to gather my thoughts in the hallway, I came to realize just what had been transpiring all this time. Sadie had wanted to go somewhere where my little ambulette couldn't take her.

Sadie's hope and faith promised her a place where everything would be made new; where the old had passed away. Sadie believed that because of Jesus' death on the cross and His resurrection; there would be a new Jerusalem; a new Heaven; a new Earth. A place where there would be no sin. A place where death, pain and suffering would be no more. She believed that Jesus was with her in the beginning; was with her all her life; and would be there at the end. Jesus is the Alpha and the Omega. The Beginning and the End.

Sadie showed me in her own way that this world is not the one where I should be putting my priorities. She showed me that there is another world promised to me, far beyond anything I could possibly imagine. In retrospect; I wish somehow that I could turn back the hands of time. I wish that I could hear once again that gravelly voice asking me; "Hey mister; soon there?" I would immediately pull my little van off to the side of the road. I would take her hands in mine and look straight and unflinchingly into her eyes. Then with all the courage and conviction I could muster, I would say those words she so desperately wanted to hear:

"Yes Sadie…soon there." "Soon there, Sadie!"

Thanks be to God!

Alan Vandewater
May 9, 2004

Revelation 21: vs 1-6

1 Then I saw a new heaven and a new earth; for the first heaven and the first earth had passed away, and the sea was no more. 2 And I saw the new the holy city, the new Jerusalem, coming down out of heaven from God, prepared as a bride for her husband. 3 And I heard a loud voice from the throne saying, "See, the home of God is among mortals. He will dwell with them; they will be his peoples, and God himself will be with them; 4 he will wipe every tear from their eyes. Death will be no more; mourning and crying and pain will be no more, for the first things have passed away."5 And the one who was seated on the throne said, "See, I am making all things new." Also, he said, "Write this for the words are trustworthy and true." 6 Then he said to me, "It is done! I am the Alpha and the Omega, the beginning and the end. To the thirsty I will give water as a gift from the spring of the water of life."

"Humility and Hospitality"

Last Summer I went to a wedding just outside New York City. My best friend's son was getting married. Having watched him grow up I was indeed honored to have been invited. I packed my best black pants, my black dress shoes, black socks and a crisp white button-down dress shirt, along with a nice necktie. I thought I would look rather spiffy for an afternoon Summer event. All was well until I unpacked my suitcase. Apparently rough handling had caused the ball point pen in my suitcase to disgorge all its contents onto several belongings, including my crisp white dress shirt. The only solution in mind was to try to find a replacement first thing the next day, which was exactly what I tried to do. After trying all day at various merchants to find a satisfactory replacement; the only thing I could find was a very presentable, quality made, white golf shirt. Although it wasn't exactly what I had wanted, I still felt decently dressed.

All these good thoughts disappeared as soon as I got to the ceremony. There to my dismay, I found that not only were white shirts and ties the order of the day for male guests; but that jackets were expected to be worn also. This day was not starting out well for me at all! I could discern some impolite murmurs pointed my way as I sat through the ceremony with my friend's mother. Later, as I made my way through the rather elegant appetizer buffet line, I could just feel other people's eyes shadowing me. They were trying to figure out whether I was a guest, some sort of security, or if I was part of the restaurant management group. All of this was making me very uncomfortable indeed. As we entered the grand ballroom for the main dinner, I found that it wasn't at all over with for me. Even being at one of the furthest tables from the hosts, among some friends that I knew, didn't calm my uneasiness at all.

"Why are all these people making opinions of me?" "Don't they know that I am friends with the host too?" Besides, they didn't know the whole story. They didn't know what had transpired, and how I had done my very best to rectify the situation. I had tried my very best to fix something that I had had no control over. Finally, I had the chance to pull my host aside and apologize, and explain the reason why I wasn't exactly following protocol.

He listened intently and then put his hands on my shoulders and said, "I couldn't care less what you are wearing." "It's not important." "What is important is that you are an honored guest of mine, at my son's wedding. You are here because of who you are and what you are – my best friend – and that is all that matters." "Now, come with me; there are some out-of-state firefighters that I'd like you to meet." Feeling a whole lot better, I set off with him.

I was indeed thankful that my friend didn't admonish me and dispatch me to a far corner. I was thankful that he liked me for who I was, and for his wisdom in not letting a breach of protocol ruin twenty-five years of friendship. I was indeed a very lucky man to have a host like him.

In the Bible, Jesus says: "For all who exalt themselves will be humbled, and those who humble themselves will be exalted." This verse from Luke's Gospel explains that we shouldn't be haughty and full of ourselves, lest the situation come to a point where we find we aren't as pompous and important as we thought. Then you will get relegated to a lesser position and with a less important seat. Sometimes, we as church people act the way the other guests did to me at this wedding. We claim that we want to be accepting of all people, but when it comes to actually doing this, we find that we are as judgmental as those people were to me.

There comes a time in many congregations, especially in rural areas, when we simply can't rely on the family element to keep us going. What used to be pews filled with generations of various families isn't the case anymore. More and more congregations find themselves seeking out new ways to increase their membership. This is a strange new concept for many. We find ourselves reaching out more and more to strangers, in hopes of expanding our flock. But what if these strangers, especially in some towns, aren't exactly what we were expecting?

What would we do if a woman came in wearing clothes that were mismatched, or even "out of season?" What if a man entered and had a two-day growth of beard that made him appear slovenly and lazy? Or perhaps a young lady comes in who has a disability which, despite her best efforts, causes her to be the center of attention?" How would we handle these possible scenarios? Would we see these people based upon first appearances only and make snap judgments? Would we treat them like the people did to me at my friend's wedding; even though we don't know all the details surrounding that person?

Would we be polite, but not push our welcome "too hard"? Would we rationalize that maybe they'd be there for an hour and then we'd never see them again? If that happened we could always say; "Well, we did our best."

There shouldn't be any class distinctions at any banquet, or the most important banquet of them all: "The Eucharist." We should take care to know all the particulars before we form opinions of others.

Perhaps the mismatched woman wore the only clothes she could afford, because she spent all her funds to make sure her children had what they needed first. Perhaps the man with the stubble has a skin condition which, until it heals, means that he cannot shave and make himself presentable. Perhaps the young disabled woman has seen her condition worsen because of the side effects of the only medicine that will help her in the long run. We should help all of those who come to us seeking solace, in any way we can.

It takes guts and courage to come to a place you've never been to before. It takes an enormous amount of fortitude to seek someone's help out of need, in spite of not "measuring up." Desperation and desire make people do whatever it takes. We should invite strangers to this place and to the Lord's banquet and make them feel really welcome. Not only because we will get something in return, but because it is the right thing to do.

In verse 13 of Luke 14, Jesus says in essence that when we give a banquet, we should invite "the poor, the lame, the crippled and the blind." Then He says, "You will be blessed even though they cannot repay you because you will be repaid at the Resurrection of the righteous." Like my friend, Jesus as the host wants us as honored guests at His banquet because of who we are, and what we are: His children.

Jesus humbled Himself and humiliated Himself, and died on the cross so that we would all be equal. So that we could all partake of His holy meal together. So that we would all have access to eternal life with God, through Him, and not be judged by our inadequacies. If God can do this to us wretched people, how can we possibly take it upon ourselves to judge others? Jesus commanded us to "love one another" but he puts it in a context that leaves no doubt as to how encompassing our love should be. "Love one another, as I have loved you." Everyone is invited to the Lord's banquet regardless of their perceived status.

Thanks be to God!

Alan G. Vandewater
August 29, 2004

Luke 14: 1 and 7-14

1 On one occasion when Jesus was going to the house of a leader of the Pharisees to eat a meal on the sabbath, they were watching him closely. 7 When he noticed how the guests chose the places of honor, he told them a parable.8 "When you are invited by someone to a wedding banquet, do not sit down at the place of honor, in case someone more distinguished than you has been invited by your host 9 and the host who invited both of you may come to you and say to you, "Give this person your place," and then in disgrace you would start to take the lowest place. 10 But when you are invited, go and sit down at the lowest place, so that when your host comes, he may say to you, "Friend, move up higher;" then you will be honored in the presence of all who sit at the table with you. 11 For all who exalt themselves will be humbled and those who humble themselves will be exalted."12 He said also to the one who had invited him, "When you give a luncheon or a dinner do not invite your friends or your brothers or your relatives or rich neighbors, in case they may invite you in return, and you would be repaid. 13 But when you give a banquet, invite the poor, the crippled, the lame and the blind. 14 And you will be blessed, because they cannot repay you, for you will be repaid at the resurrection of the righteous."

"Forgive and Forget"

Before we begin our service this morning, I would like to have each of you shake the hand of the person next to you. Good; didn't that feel wonderful? Don't you wish that it could be that pleasant all the time? But what would you have done if the person next to you was someone who had hurt you in the past, or was your enemy? Would you have still done the same?

In today's Gospel, Jesus says to us:

> "but if you love those who love you, what credit is that to you?" "For even sinners, love those who love them." "And if you do good to those who do good to you; what credit is that to you?" "For even sinners do the same." "Be merciful, just as your Father is merciful." "Forgive and you will be forgiven."

I've been thinking that maybe this "forgiveness" thing needs a little more study and insight. You've all heard of or played the board game Scrabble, haven't you? This is a game where you put letter tiles on a rack in front of you and try to arrange and rearrange the letters to get the combination that is best for you. Now let's put them aside for just a few moments and study this forgiveness thing a little further.

The phrase "forgive and forget." How often we've heard those words. They are usually proclaimed by a third person, trying to bring an end to an ongoing controversy. So why does it oftentimes seem to come out in the reverse, as in "forget to forgive?" Did we really forget? Or is it that we find that we just can't? Or worse yet, we won't!

How many of us remember as kids, when one of our parents would get really mad at us, for the same thing, sometimes after the third or fourth offense? They would then send us off to our rooms with parting words, something like: "and don't you dare come out, until I say you can!" After the initial shame of being caught had sunk in and as we were being punished, reality set in. We then started to really think about what we did and began to wonder. Would they forget? Would they forgive? Would things ever get back the way they were? We yearned for the inner peace and the good feeling of being loved.

What about the parents? Were they not also aching? They had to do the right thing in disciplining you because they had to, not because they wanted to. Of course, they forgave and forgot. They also wanted that inner peace and the good feelings that forgiveness would produce.

Let's get back to our imaginary game. We've started with the word "forget" on our rack, but I think we can do better than that. A better, bigger word is "forgive." We see that to forgive is good, but we don't actually forgive. How come? In a similar vein, talk show host Dr. Laura Schlessinger says: "The Ten Commandments are not prefaced by the words, "When you're in the mood." We see that it also goes with learning to forgive. You don't forgive only when you're in the mood. You don't forgive only when it's to your advantage. You don't forgive only when it doesn't hurt too much.

When we forgive, we free ourselves from those awful feelings that bind us to the one who hurt us. We need to rise above the pettiness that keeps us at the same level as them. So, let's replace our six-letter word, "forget" with the seven-letter word, "forgive."

When we say the Lord's Prayer, we acknowledge who God is and that His name shall be hallowed. We then petition Him for several things. Among these is the petition that He forgive us our trespasses, as we forgive those who trespass against us. "Wait a minute!" Didn't we just say, "as we forgive those who trespass against us"? We ask God to be our forgiver, but are we keeping up our end of the bargain? Let's replace our seven-letter word, "forgive" with the eight-letter word, "forgiver." To be a forgiver, we need to acknowledge that we have many faults of our own. We need to take a good look inwards and realize that it could very well be ourselves who would need to be forgiven; if the course of events were reversed. Being that both the words forgiver and forgiven are equal in number; let's add another letter and explore the word "forgiving."

To be forgiving is not always easy. Sometimes we just can't. Sometimes it hurts too much. Sometimes the wounds just won't heal enough to be able to bring closure; to bring forgiveness. Sometimes we need the help of a Higher Power. To be forgiving needs to come from the heart. It needs to come from the hearts of all involved. It cannot be faked. It cannot be contrived. It needs to be true. This leads us to a new eleven letter word; "forgiveness." It is the biggest, best word we've put together so far. To get to this word means that we had to work very hard at it.

Ultimately; forgiveness is what everyone is after. Forgiveness brings peace. Forgiveness makes us whole. Unmitigated forgiveness sets us free.

Today we found that in the Game of Life, as with the board game, forgiveness is not an easily reached objective. It takes love, unselfishness and heart. It takes pain. It takes sacrifice.

Every year we celebrate Easter. With each observance, we will be painfully reminded just how much love, unselfishness, sacrifice, heart and pain is required to forgive. We will understand the sacrifice that our Father in Heaven made. Where He gave up his only Son, for our forgiveness from sin. This was done by grace, not only to cover our transgressions in the past, but in the future and forevermore.

It seems that forgiveness is our longest word.
Forgiveness is our best word option.
Forgiveness, whether we are giving it or getting it;
is a wonderful way to win the game!

Thanks be to God!

Alan Vandewater
February 18, 2001

Luke 6: 32-36

32 "If you love those who love you, what credit is that to you? For even sinners love those who love them.33 If you do good to those who do good to you, what credit is that to you? For even sinners do the same. 34 If you lend to those from whom you hope to receive, what credit is that to you? Even sinners lend to sinners, to receive as much again. 35 But love your enemies, do good, and lend expecting nothing in return. Your reward will be great, and you will be children of the Most High; for he is kind to the ungrateful and the wicked. 36 Be merciful, just as your Father is merciful.

"Use Them or Lose Them"

We hear the term "use them or lose them" a lot at this time of year.

- Use your insurance benefits...or lose them.
- Take your vacation days...or lose them.
- Use your IRA and tax benefits...or lose them.

Seems like everyone is on our case about using them or losing them. How ironic that at this, the end of the church year, we relate the story of how even Jesus wants us to use the things we have...or lose them.

In the Gospels we hear the word "talents" mentioned frequently. Jesus speaks to the disciples using a scenario that they can relate to, like He does in almost all His parables. Jesus talks about God's gifts by using a monetary unit called a talent to emphasize his point about how great God's gifts to us are.

Just to put some context to all this so that it makes sense, let me explain how this works:

The "shekel" was the lowest form of currency in use.
It took FIFTY shekels to equal one Mina.
After THREE month's work, you might earn TEN Minas.
It took EIGHTEEN MONTHS of work, or SIXTY Minas to equal just ONE Talent!

The talent was the highest-valued currency used in Ancient Rome. As you can see, this is a considerable amount of money, and yet it is the lowest denomination we hear about in Jesus' parable. Because of its worth, it has evolved in today's language to mean abilities, or something special, as in God-given talents. I am now going to illustrate this story using characters that we can relate to today.

Just a few weeks ago our local High School Football team closed out a spectacular season by capturing its second crown in as many years. It was indeed a determined and talented team.

One player, the wide receiver, must have had the five talents. He could dodge, twist and outrun his opponents with ease. He added to that by being able to kick field goals, which bettered his teams scores even more. I would say his talents were used well, based on the team's success.

Another player, the quarterback, was no slouch either. He called the plays, took the hikes, and while back-stepping, managed to elude all his opponents. All the while he was watching for eligible receivers downfield. His passes, more often than not, were completions. This added to the team's successes also. I would say that he, too, used his talents wisely. Each of the players, though different, doubled his reward by using the talent that he had.

Our man on the frontline hasn't been forgotten either. He received just one talent, based on his responsibility and his capabilities. Let's face it. There are only so many things a 250 lb. guy can do in the long term. He can't run; he can't pass; but he can block! This man took his talent and his responsibility and made the most of it. Every time the ball was hiked, he crashed into the man in front of him, oblivious to what was happening around him. He was doing his job to the best of his ability and because of his help, all the other components worked well together. The coach was a very happy man indeed!

But suppose, like the man in our Gospel reading, the lineman decided that his one talent was an injustice. He felt that he was mistreated and was passed over. He then decided that it wasn't worth doing anything with, or perhaps he felt having just one talent didn't amount to much; and so, there wasn't a whole lot he could do with it. He decided not to do anything with it and not take chances that might land him in trouble. He decided to just not do anything and play it safe.

On each consecutive play, the lineman stood passively idle when the ball was hiked. Of course, nothing was accomplished by the other players either, because the opposing team was simply charging through the now wide-open hole! Needless to say, the coach was no longer a happy man. He snatched the only talent the player had, and after kicking him off the team gave that talent to the man who had already earned ten. The coach couldn't understand why the lineman hadn't done something; so, he dismissed him for not doing so.

God wants us to use His gifts wisely. He does not take lightly someone who takes these gifts and doesn't do anything with them, no matter how small. Jesus indicates that merely maintaining things as they are, is not sufficient.

God gave each of us gifts and talents according to our capabilities and responsibilities. Therefore, we have the responsibility to our Lord, to each other and to ourselves to allow the Holy Spirit to work within us. That we use God's gifts to the utmost of our abilities. That we build up the body of Christ. That we strive to serve those who suffer injustice. That we share our riches and God's love with each other. As the Bible says about our "talents."

> "If your gift is to prophesy, then use it as your faith tells you to."
> "If it is Administration, then use it for administration."

"If it is for teaching, then use it for teaching."
"Let the preachers, deliver sermons."
"The almsgivers, give freely."
"The Officials to be diligent."
"and to those who do the works of mercy, let them do so cheerfully."

So, maybe we now realize that we've been a little lax in moving forward, in using the gifts God has given us, to our best ability. "What's the rush?" we ask. "We have plenty of time left." Like the man who left the country and entrusted his servants to act accordingly while he was gone; Jesus too will return!

We say in our prayers:

"Help us to prepare for the world to come;
doing the work which you have given us to do;
while it is day, before that night comes when
no one can work."

We say these words fervently and yet we don't always seem to act on them. We cannot; and will not know the hour of the Lord's return. We need to watch and be ready. Mothers constantly admonish their children about what to do and how and when, and mine was no different. Even on her funeral card she left this message for me;

"There is work still waiting for you;
you must not idly stand."
"Do it now while life remaineth;
you shall rest in Jesus' land."
"And when that is all completed;
 He will gently call you home."

I remember her memory and God's intent by doing what I'm doing today, in God's honor and to all that I can and use my talents to the utmost, whatever they may be.

We need to get working now; to use our abilities as best we can, no matter how inconsequential we feel they are. This way we can meet with Jesus on the last day and be joyful and full of "Hallelujahs" and not disgrace and despair.

We need to remember that old adage about our abilities and talents:

"Use them or lose them."

Thanks be to God!

Alan Vandewater
November 17, 2002

Matthew 25:14-30

14 For it is as if a man, going on a journey, summoned his slaves and entrusted his property to them; 15 to one he gave five talents, to another two, to another one, to each according to his ability. Then he went away. 16 The one who had received the five talents went off at once and traded with them, and made five more talents. 17 In the same way, the one who had the two talents made two more talents. 18 But the one who had received the one talent went off and dug a hole in the ground and hid his master's money. 19 After a long time the master of those slaves came and settled accounts with them. 20 Then the one who had received the five talents came forward, bringing five more talents, saying, "Master, you handed over to me five talents; see, I have made five more talents." 21 His master said to him "Well done good and trustworthy slave; you have been trustworthy in a few things, I will put you in charge of many things; enter into the joy of your master."22 And the one with the two talents also came forward saying, "Master,

you handed over to me two talents; see, I have made two more talents." 23 His master said to him, "Well done, good and trustworthy slave; you have been trustworthy in a few things, I will put you in charge of many things; enter into the joy of your master." 24 Then the one who had received the one talent also came forward, saying, "Master, I knew that you were a harsh man, reaping where you did not sow, and gathering where you did not scatter seed; 25 so I was afraid, and I went and hid the your talent in the ground." "Here you have what is yours." 26 But his master replied, "You wicked and lazy slave! You knew, did you, that I reap where I did not sow, and gather where I did not scatter?" 27 "Then you ought to have invested my money with the bankers, and on my return I would have received what was my own, with interest." 28 "So take that talent from him, and give it to the one with the ten talents." 29 For to all those who have, more will be given, and they will have an abundance; but from those who have nothing, even what they have will be taken away. 30 As for this worthless slave, throw him in the outer darkness, where there will be weeping and the gnashing of teeth.

"When Will the World End?"

We've all seen cartoons showing an old man wearing a white robe and sporting a long beard, who is carrying around a sign around that says either; "The end is near." or more specifically; "The world will end tomorrow." We put our hands over our mouths and snicker at what we deem to be utter foolishness. The world's not going to end any time soon. "That's crazy!" Besides, we don't really want to think about that possibility right now.

Could it be that we don't want to think about this now because we've got our own selfish desires that we're concerned about? We've got things to do! Grandkids to spoil, families to raise, careers to start, retirement to think about, Cadillac cars, and luxury vacations! "Nah." We don't want to think about the end. We're having too much fun now; or maybe the reason is because we're not really sure at all about this dying thing. But how do we know that the guy with the signs isn't right? How come we can't quite dismiss what's in the back of our minds?

Mark's Gospel warns that there will be "wars and rumors of war; nation against nation; kingdom against kingdom; earthquakes and famine." All these things have happened before and are still happening. In addition, we have wildfires, global warming, health epidemics and pandemics. We have people bent on destroying each other including despots armed with nuclear devices that could annihilate entire populations. Maybe the nuts with the signs are right. Maybe the end is getting near! But then again, we reason, all of this has transpired before and we're still here, right?

Even though we've been through the calamities mentioned previously, and are still here, how do we know for sure that God's plan won't make the next one the "definitive" one? Speculating on "the end of the world" is fruitless. No one knows the end time except the Father. Not us, not the angels, not Jesus...only the Father! We don't know; and therein lies the good and the bad.

As Mark relates in his Gospel, Jesus takes the "inner circle" of disciples, consisting of Simon Peter, Andrew, James and John, up on the Mount of Olives to have a discussion with them. This in is direct contrast to the many times Jesus has met them by the shore, surrounded by crowds. This must be really important.

The location of the Mount is on the east side of the temple, and the fact that it is higher reinforces the fact that that the Temple is not the reigning, supreme fixture that everyone believes it to be. The Temple has been there for thousands of years, but it has become "unholy" and will be destroyed. Jesus wants to figuratively point out that there are more important things to come. Though the destruction of the Temple is not a sign of the coming of the Messiah; from this point on (for Christians) the coming of "The Son of Man" in glory replaces the Temple as a focus of hope. It is the full realization of the kingdom of God. The intention is to call the followers of Jesus to hope for the coming of the "Son of Man." This hope will sustain Christians undergoing persecution. It will strengthen them to "endure to the end." Jesus warns the disciples of the trials to come and also upon the world. Jesus exhorts them to "not be alarmed."

Hope is the one reason we can look beyond the "doom and gloom" and all the predictions. Hope is what we have because of Jesus' actions. Christ offered Himself as a sacrifice; so that sinners who have been cleansed by His blood might have Eternal Life. Non- Christians do not understand this concept.

Franklin Delano Roosevelt, one of our past Presidents, during especially tumultuous days said: "The only thing we have to fear, is fear itself." Those who don't believe, fear. Those who have hope have no fear. Christ gave once and for all for our sins. If we have hope and faith, who cares what the signs say?

As we keep dismissing the messages of the guy with the signs, the question still remains; "When will the end times come for us?" We don't know when the Lord will come. We don't know if it will be at midnight, or when the cock crows, or somewhere in between. We have been admonished to not fall asleep and not be ready, but to be alert, be ready and "watch." There are some who interpret "watch" as to expect the literal return of Jesus Christ in the immediate future. Those who point to this theory, identify current events spoken in verses 5-23 and say, "Now is the time." Others take seriously the warning that the time is unknown (verse 32) and insist that Jesus is coming "very soon." A third option exists where we understand the return of "The Son of Man" as per one's experiences. This could come as a resolution of one's severe trials, or as a divine intervention or even at the end of one's life. It matters not, which of the three motivates us into action, as long as we realize the implications of how it will affect us. Regardless of when we feel the end times will come, we as believers are armed against the wiles of the deceivers. We are sustained through any suffering or persecution we might endure. It motivates us to get on with the mission to "make disciples of all nations."

Hope builds up our daily life by making each moment we live, subject to the coming of the "Son of Man" who comes to judge and save. We can use this time to do good. We can practice love and good deeds. We can keep reaching out to encourage one another. We can continue to earnestly spread the Gospel.

As we wait for the day to come, we can strive to keep ourselves pure and with a clean heart. Then we can approach the kingdom of God with a full confession of faith and the assurance of hope.

Maybe collectively, the guy with the signs is right. Maybe the end is near, or maybe it will end tomorrow. It might even come later than that, but we don't care! We don't fear. Instead we have confidence and hope, because Jesus did it all for us; once and for all time. Eternal life is ours when He comes. So, let us be ready. Let us be watchful. Let us be awake.

Thanks be to God!

Alan Vandewater
November 19,2006

Mark 13: 1-8

1 As he came out of the temple, one of the disciples said to him, "Look, Teacher, what large stones and what large buildings!" 2 Then Jesus asked him, "Do you see these great buildings? Not one stone will be left here upon another; all will be thrown down." 3 When he was sitting on the Mount of Olives opposite the temple, Peter, James, John, and Andrew asked him privately, 4 "Tell us, when will this be, and what will be the sign that all of these things are about to be accomplished?" 5 Then Jesus began to say to them, "Beware that no one leads you astray. 6 Many will come in my name and say, I am he! And they will lead many astray. 7 When you hear of wars and rumors of wars, do not be alarmed; this must take place, but the end is still to come. 8 For nation will rise against nation, and kingdom against kingdom; there will be earthquakes in various places; there will be famines. This is but the beginning of the birth pangs.

"A Quiet Time... A Quiet Gift"

One of my most favorite gifts is one my Mom gave me for Christmas a month after I joined the Fire Department at age twenty-one. It is an enlargement of a picture taken sixteen years before when I was just a kid at five. There I was wearing my father's uniform hat, perched precariously on my head, and wearing an obviously way too big Fire Department jacket with the Maltese Cross emblazoned on the chest. But the biggest, most telling factor, of this occasion, was the ear-to-ear grin of a boy obviously proud and honored to be a part of this innocuous photo session. Who would've thought that a tiny 2"x 2" photo would be a sign of things to come?

I used to watch Dad peel away from the curb, racing to the firehouse to catch the truck. There I stood; the proud son in an envious neighborhood. Later when I had a bike, I would pedal furiously to the juncture of the roads where I could watch the trucks head southward to the call. Later on, smarter and wiser, I would count the air horn blasts, look them up in a coded alarm book, and go directly to the scene if it was at all feasible. All this time I'd kept looking in the photo album at the tiny picture. I knew that the day was coming when I would be a "grown up" version of the little kid in the picture, uniform and all.

Being a young mother, my Mom had other concerns on her mind besides the innocent photo of her firstborn son. But she couldn't ignore the signs as they kept popping up. I'm sure as time passed, she became more concerned about where this might be leading. She treasured what other people said and pondered them all in her heart. She tried to make sense of something she didn't completely understand.

There was no doubt by this time that I was going to end up on a mission. A mission to help people and to save lives. A mission that was dangerous. A mission that might bring me injury and a very good possibility of death; and there was nothing in her power that my Mom could do to stop it. So, she did the best she could, this young mom, to raise her son and his siblings the best she knew how. She protected me and loved me with all her heart and was faithful always to instill God's will in me. In the Bible we read of another young mother, whose son is also destined for a mission. She too, is mulling over the signs she is receiving, surrounding her firstborn son.

First, an angel appears with the news that through the Holy Spirit, she will become pregnant and carry Jesus, God's only Son. Then in a dream, God guides Joseph into doing the right thing and marrying Mary, the expectant mother. Then quietly the miraculous birth occurs. Then the shepherds and wise men come rejoicing in the good news and honor the newborn king. But King Herod seeks to kill the newborn babe; and God warns Joseph in another dream to escape quietly into the night, to Egypt to keep the child from danger. Finally, again quietly, in a dream, the couple get the okay that it is safe to return to Judea, but instead they settle in their hometown of Nazareth, in Galilee.

"A quiet time… a quiet gift."

Mary, like my Mom, treasures everything that is being said about her son. She ponders them in her heart, not fully understanding the mission, the truth. She does the best she can, with all her hopes and fears, to protect her child, to love him with all her heart, to raise him up according to "the law." To always do God's will as a faithful servant and as a good parent.

Today's reading finds the couple in Jerusalem, fulfilling their obligations under Jewish law by presenting their son to the Lord and offering their sacrifices. If there were any doubts left as to their son's importance, they were vanquished forever upon entering the Temple and encountering a prophet named Simeon. According to accounts, Simeon takes Jesus in his arms and praises God with joy, for letting him see the Messiah before he dies, as God has promised him. Simeon then says; "Mine eyes have seen your salvation, which you have prepared in the presence of all peoples." "A light for revelation to the Gentiles, and for glory to your people Israel." Simeon adds that "the child will be responsible for the rising and falling of many in Israel; and to be opposed; and a sword will pierce Mary's own soul also."

As if this wasn't enough, Anna the prophetess breaks her years of fasting and unceasing prayer, by coming to the Christ child. She then begins to praise God also with joy. She begins speaking about the child to all those present who were seeking the redemption of Israel; saying: "For those who have lived in darkness; have seen a great light."

The parents wondrously took this all in and did what they were required to do and then returned to their hometown. There they watched their child grow strong, filled with wisdom, and the favor of God was upon him. The Bible doesn't say how Mary felt about these proclamations that were again reinforcing her fears.

The only thing she could do was to follow God's will. God and His will are real, and He acts no matter how we feel about it. God is Emmanuel and He is present with us, no matter what the circumstance may be.

Death, illness, loss of jobs, war and poverty are only a few of the things that can make the "Merry" in Christmas, not so "merry." It also takes the "Happy" out of our New Year's. Our warped vision of happiness depends on things going our way. Joy, as we saw from Simeon and Anna, happens when God is present, as we saw when they proclaimed it to all who were there. Joy comes from the certain knowledge of our Lord's abiding presence, then and even now.

I thought the simple gift my Mother gave me that Christmas so many years ago was the best present I could've ever received. I'm sure you've had your absolute best gifts too. But we shouldn't dwell so much on the presents that are materialistic and will lose their importance. Rejoice instead on the gift that God gave us one Christmas, long, long ago. The gift that lasts forever. The gift of Jesus. The gift of eternal life. The gift of joy to the world. Mothers may see the signs; but God the Father controls the outcome.

"A quiet time…a quiet gift."

Thanks be to God!

Alan Vandewater
December 29, 2002

Luke 2: 22-40

22 When the time came for their purification, according to the law of Moses, they brought him up to Jerusalem to present him to the Lord. 23 (as it written in the law of the Lord, "Every firstborn male shall be designated as holy to the Lord") 24 and they offered a sacrifice according to what is stated in the law of the Lord." "a pair of turtledoves or two young pigeons." 25 Now there was man in Jerusalem whose name was Simeon; this man was righteous and devout, looking forward to

the consolation of Israel, and the Holy Spirit rested on him. 26 It had been revealed to him by the Holy Spirit that he would not see death before he had seen the Lord's Messiah. 27 Guided by the Spirit, Simeon came into the temple; and when the parents brought in the child Jesus, to do for him what was customary under the law, 28 Simeon took him in his arms and praised God, saying, 29 "Master, now you are dismissing your servant in peace, according to your word; 30 for mine eyes have seen your salvation 31 which you prepared in the presence of all your peoples, 32 a light for revelation to the Gentiles and for glory to your people Israel." 33 And the child's father and mother were amazed at what was being said about him. 34 Then Simeon blessed them and said to his mother Mary, "This child is destined for the failing and the rising of many in Israel, and to be a sign that will be opposed 35 so that the inner thoughts of many will be revealed—and a sword will "pierce your own soul too."36 There was also a prophet, Anna, the daughter of Phanuel, of the tribe of Asher. She was of a great age having lived with her husband seven years after their marriage, 37 then as a widow to the age of eighty-four. She never left the temple but worshipped there night and day. 38 At that moment she came and began to praise God and to speak about the child to all who were looking for the redemption of Jerusalem. 39 When they had finished everything required by the law of the Lord, they returned to Galilee, to their own town of Nazareth. 40 The child grew and became strong, filled with wisdom; and the favor of God was upon him.

"It Isn't Time Yet"

People who know me know of my aversion to early morning hours. I would rather do anything at four, five, or six p.m. then at four, five, or six in the morning! In my younger years I thought nothing of still being on the go late at night, sometimes not crawling into bed until the wee hours of the morning. The fact that it was now Christmas Eve and that I was married didn't seem to make much of a difference. It was always the early mornings that dealt me the harsh realities.

I remember Christmas mornings when my children would bounce on the bed somewhere around five in the morning, demanding that we get up and see what had transpired the night before. Having only retired shortly before, and with only a few hours' rest, more sleep was not only desirable but a necessity. "It's not time yet!" I would say. "We'll all enjoy our presents more if we just wait until it's time." Now I ask you: what kind of father would tell his children,

"It isn't time yet"?

In Matthew's Gospel lesson today, we learn that the wise men have left Bethlehem and are returning to their homelands. We also learn of the angel appearing in a dream, instructing Joseph to take the mother and child and immediately depart for Egypt. This was because King Herod, with his insecurities and lust for power, has ordered all the babes two years and younger in Bethlehem and surrounding areas to be killed. This would ensure that no "new king" would replace him on the throne. Joseph took the family to Egypt as ordered, fulfilling, as some say, God's prophecy through the prophet Jeremiah: "Out of Egypt I have called my Son."

Matthew uses this Old Testament reference to imply that all was not lost for Israel due to the slaying of the innocent babes. He lets us know that Jesus' escape to Egypt will bring happiness and hope to all, in spite of man's atrocities.

Another reference in Matthew from Hosea, (another prophet) says: "When Israel was a child; I loved Him and out of Egypt, I have called my Son." Everyone thinks that Herod swooped down to kill all the babes within a few days of Jesus' birth. Not so. The great reformer, Martin Luther, puts things differently. According to him, as the wise men were leaving Jesus, Herod, a Roman appointee over the territory in question, finds himself in Rome on official business.

Joseph and Mary being dutiful parents and citizens; went to Jerusalem to observe the post-birth ritual and to sacrifice two doves. Mary spent forty days purifying herself. The Christ-child was circumcised and was presented to Anna and Simeon in the Temple. All these things needed to be done before they could return to their home. When Herod comes back from his trip to Rome, he has no clear idea of when the Christ child was born; therefore, he issues the overarching decree that all children under the age of two must be slaughtered to protect his reign. This is when the angel appears and tells the Holy Family to leave and go immediately to Egypt.

"It isn't time yet."

Many years later, Joseph again receives God's word through an angel also in a dream. God tells Joseph that it is safe to return to their homeland, that those who sought the child's life are dead. However, Archelaus, one of Herod's sons, is now the new ruler of Judea; and he is just as ruthless as his father was. Joseph then decides to move to Galilee instead, where another, much more tolerant son named Antipas rules. This fulfills another prophecy that Jesus would be a Nazarene. It is also interesting to note that Nazareth is in Galilee, a predominantly Gentile region. This firmly establishes Jesus as being without a doubt, the Savior of the world. His Gospel for the kingdom is open to all peoples.

John the Baptist, in the Gospel of John, tells us that "in the beginning was the Word, and the Word was with God." "He was there in the beginning and all things came into being through Him." I wonder why, if He was the Life, why didn't He come sooner?

"It isn't time yet."

As we've mentioned before, our human race was intent on doing things our way. We thought our way was best. We ignored and almost forgot about God and His directives. Eventually we drifted further and further and forgot God completely. But God didn't forget us! God loved us so much that He sent His only begotten Son to die for us, so we would be free from sin and be able to rest eternally in Heaven. John came to extol all non-believers that soon the light (Jesus) would come. The one through whom all life would be enlightened. God's plan was to have Jesus grow to maturity, turn the people around, and teach them hope and repentance.

"It isn't time yet."

We need to remember that God moves in His own time, and not according to ours. We recount the dreams that came to the Holy Family. The warnings, the instructions, the timelines. These were all part of God's plan to keep the Christ-child alive. All were aimed at keeping the prophecies alive, as written in the Scriptures. Now we find ourselves reading about the time in life where Jesus has matured and surpassed childhood. But there are still those who want to kill him.

Years later, Jesus finds himself betrayed. He is sentenced to die, after suffering horrendous torture, suffering and humiliation. This time it was started by the Jewish elite who were the ones fearing the loss of power, not power-hungry kings.

"Where were all the angelic choirs then?"
"Where were the dreams, whispered in
the night to escape?"
"Where was the rejoicing and resounding
joy of previous times?"
"Where were His friends; to warn Him of
danger and to guide Him away?"

The time was getting near for Jesus' arrest and crucifixion. The people still didn't understand. They were as far turned away from God as they had ever been. God's present was about to be delivered. Jesus' birth was only the starting point. Jesus needed to die to fulfill the Scriptures, and to redeem us and to free us from sin. Jesus submitted Himself to the will of the Father. He surrendered Himself on the cross for the benefit of all mankind.

"Now it was time."

What would be the scenario? Would we still be there, listening for our Father to say when it was time, unlike the people of that day? Would we wait patiently to get the greatest present of all time, or would we have gotten impatient and turned away? Would we feed our own desires first; therefore missing out on this great gift completely?

What kind of father would say to his children that it "wasn't time yet?" What kind of father would ask his children to wait, saying they would enjoy the present more "when it was time?"

A loving Father, that's who. One who knows His children best.

Thanks be to God!

Alan Vandewater
January 2, 2005

Matthew 2: 13-23

Now when they had left, an angel of the Lord appeared to Joseph in a dream and said, "Get up, take the child and His mother and flee to Egypt and remain there until I tell you; for Herod is about to search for the child, to destroy him." Then Joseph got up, took the child and his mother by night and went to Egypt, and remained there until the death of Herod. This was to fulfill what had been spoken by the Lord through the prophet, "Out of Egypt I have called my son."

When Herod saw that he had been tricked by the wise men, he was infuriated, and he went and killed all the children in and around Bethlehem, who were two years old and under, according to the time that he had learned from the wise men. Then was fulfilled what had been spoken through the prophet, Jeremiah: "A voice was heard in Ramah, wailing and loud lamentation, Rachel weeping for her children: she refused to be consoled, because they are no more."

When Herod died, an angel of the Lord suddenly appeared in a dream to Joseph in Egypt and said, "Get up, take the child and his mother and go to the land of Israel, for those who were seeking the child's life are dead." Then Joseph got up and took the child and his mother and went to the land of Israel. But when he heard that Archelaus was ruling over Judea in place of his father Herod, he was afraid to go there. And being warned in a dream, he went away to the district of Galilee. There he made his home in a town called Nazareth, so that what had been spoken through the prophets might be fulfilled, "He will be called a Nazarene."

"The Millennium Message"

"Well, we made it!" We made it all the way from the first day after Thanksgiving, to the first day after Christmas. We made it through all the post-Thanksgiving sales, the office parties, the family get-togethers and all the other formalities. We decorated our houses, trimmed our trees, we bought all our gifts and placed them under the decorated branches. Then we waited anxiously for the big guy to arrive; Santa Claus, himself.

In our churches we had a similar experience. We set up the Advent wreath and each week we'd sing a different hymn, and light another candle. Every week we would hear a different Gospel reading, as we got closer and closer to Christmas.

Finally we got to the big night. Candles illuminated our faces as we sang "Silent Night." We celebrated the arrival of our own "big guy;" Jesus, the Christ child. What a wonderful season! Christmas is that very special time when we acknowledge the great thing that had occurred. Christmas is the celebration of the birth of God's gift to us. The beginning of our Lord's time here on Earth among us, to live with us as a human. It was the beginning of a life that would eventually lead to his death. It was an atonement for our sins; therefore making us whole with God, to receive His blessing and His forgiveness. What great news! We simply can't wait to reveal the good news to everyone who will listen! That Jesus came into this world to redeem us from the sins we do and to teach us the path to righteousness and eternal life, to be blameless before God.

I remember one hot Summer afternoon, long ago when I was a child, when my siblings and I inadvertently played

Christmas music out the nearby open window. We found that the people passing by listened with a renewed vigor. They really listened to the words playing and its meaning, because this time they weren't consumed with all the commercialism and stresses of Christmas. How refreshing and revitalizing those words sounded to them.

Now, on this day after Christmas, we pause to decide what to do with the holiday "New Year's" coming up. This is not just any year, but the start of a new millennium, two thousand years after the birth of our Lord. This is a day we set aside to make adjustments to our lives, in an attempt to make ourselves better human beings.

Let's think about this for a moment. Here we are trying to make adjustments to our lives for things that never should have happened in the first place. We have all these bad habits and things that we do that are wrong. Now; in a brief admission of guilt, we try to change these things on our own and vow never to do them again. Society tries to assist us by issuing all kinds of edicts and punishments in an attempt to keep us from doing wrong. Instead, we just keep ignoring Jesus' teachings and the Ten Commandments regularly, simply because of our greed and selfishness and failure to be concerned about our fellow man. I have heard of instances in which people have violated many of the Commandments and sometimes, all of them. Thousands of judgments, and millions of words are used, to clarify the same words that were contained so firmly and completely in the Ten Commandments.

Do we really need all these manmade rules, ordinances and regulations? Do we really need all these judges and juries, and changes and resolutions, to keep us from doing what God demands so explicitly? All we need to remember is what Jesus commanded. To paraphrase:

"That we love the Lord our God, with all our heart, and all our soul and all our mind; and that we love our neighbor as ourselves."

If we do these things as commanded; we won't have any need of resolutions to worry about. If, however, after thinking about what I said you feel the holiday just wouldn't be the same without at least one resolution, just to calm yourself, make it a resolution to start anew this year.

The choice is yours. Live as you have been, ignoring your resolutions; or live the way of Christ, and not need any resolutions, except to follow Him.

Thanks be to God!

Alan Vandewater
December 26, 2009

Deuteronomy 6: 4-5

4 Hear O Israel: The Lord is our God, the Lord alone. 5 You shall love the Lord your God with all your heart, and with all your soul, and with all your might."

PART TWO

(The Ten Years After)

Pages 75-158

"Can You Hear Me Now?"

In a commercial for a wireless phone company on TV, a man is shown walking a few steps and then asking; "Can you hear me now?" His company is putting together a telecommunications network for people to communicate with. He is testing the quality of the signal in different locations, noting where he has run into obstacles or other difficulties. He keeps testing over and over again, and each time he gets an affirmative answer to his question he simply replies, "Good!" – and moves to another location.

In this Gospel lesson from Luke, Jesus too is just starting to put together a new network. A network of communication vastly different than what we are used to, but communication just the same.

As the Gospel reveals, after being pushed back to the edge of the shore by people eager to hear His teachings, Jesus has no choice but to get into a fishing boat. He then preaches to the crowds from the water, a bit away from shore. When he is finished teaching the crowds, Jesus moves to the second phase of the day's mission. He authoritatively orders Simon Peter to put out into the deeper waters for a catch. Simon protests that they didn't have any luck the night before under optimal conditions; therefore, they weren't going to catch anything of consequence now, in the middle of a hot day. As far as Simon is concerned, Jesus may be a good carpenter and a great teacher, but Jesus isn't the fisherman that Simon is. When Jesus orders them to bring up the nets they find not one, but two nets filled to overflowing. So much so, that they were on the verge of sinking both boats due to the amount of fish that they caught.

Simon is overwhelmed by the fact, that in his sight, something amazing has just happened. This is not just some ordinary person causing all this, but someone who is extraordinary. Someone who is truly blessed. Someone unapproachable. Someone beyond measure. Realizing this, he reevaluates his own status and emphatically pleads with Jesus; "Go away from me, Lord, for I am a sinful man."

Jesus, who already knows what the end result is going to be, simply states the course of action they will be taking by saying: "Do not be afraid." "From now on, you will be catching people." Simon's protests that he isn't worthy to share space with Jesus but that doesn't bother Jesus at all. We can take a lesson from this.

Jesus isn't looking for the perfect Chief Executive. He's looking for ordinary people willing to do the work he has planned for them. People willing to "take the plunge." People willing to move forward faithfully and leave all else behind. Simon left behind a thriving fishing business, where he made money even on a slow night. Matthew the tax collector did quite well for himself also. Paul, the least of the apostles, the one who once persecuted Christians, found himself one of the most traveled of all the apostles. Jesus isn't looking for "perfect" people. He is looking for those who, for whatever their expertise or talents may be, can aid Him in growing His Church. We all have certain talents that we never thought would be of use before. We all have the potential to be disciples whether we know it or not. Maybe we just haven't heard the right words.

Jesus continues today to put together His communications network by having us spread the "Good News" of His birth, death and resurrection. When we hear that voice asking us, "Can you hear me now?" We want to be sure. We want to be confident. We want to be willing to follow Him wherever He sends us, no matter what. When Jesus asks us again; "Can you hear me now?" we want to be able to answer Him saying; "Yes" and his response will simply be: "Good!"

Thanks be to God!

Alan Vandewater
February 4, 2007

Luke 5: 1-11

1 Once while Jesus was standing by the lake of Gennesaret, and the crowd was pressing in on him to hear the word of God, 2 he saw two boats there at the shore of the lake; the fishermen had gone out of them and were washing their nets. 3 He got into one of the boats, the one belonging to Simon, and asked him to put out a little way from the shore. Then he sat down and taught the crowds from the boat. 4 When he had finished speaking, he said to Simon, "Put out into the deep water and let down your nets for a catch." 5 Simon answered, "Master, we have worked all night long but have caught nothing. Yet if you say so, I will let down the nets." 6 When they had done this, they caught so many fish that their nets were beginning to break. 7 So, they signaled their partners in the other boat to come and help them. And they came and filled both boats, so they began to sink. 8 But when Simon Peter saw it, he fell down at Jesus' knees, saying, "Go away from me, Lord, for I am a sinful man!" 9 For he and all that were with him were amazed at the catch of fish that they had taken; 10 and so also were James and John, sons of Zebedee, who were partners with Simon. Then Jesus said to Simon, "Do not be afraid; from now on you will be catching people." 11 When they had brought their boats to shore, they left everything and followed him.

"Peace Is All We Desire"

"**G**race and Peace to you from God our Father and our Lord, and Savior, Jesus Christ. (remember those words in this message.)

As most of you know the whole year from last May until now was not a very good year for me. It started with sinus surgery, which lead to pneumonia, two hospital stays, one stint in a nursing home and a whole slew of new medicines. That's not to mention doctor's appointments and the never-ending tests: one after another. This was in addition to the standard stuff every family faces at times: household bills, vehicle repairs, appliance mishaps and trying to find the time to do the things you have to do. It's enough to drive you insane, with all the demands being made of you. Really! All I want right now is a reprieve from all this, no matter how short it may be.

In about three weeks I'll get my time away. Away from the schedules, the appointments, the running around to the point where I no longer have control of my life. My chance to obtain the peace and quiet that I so desperately seek. For one solid week, I'll be listening to the crash of waves upon the shore. I'll feel the warm, gentle breezes floating over me while I sit on the balcony, resting and contemplating. I'll hit all my favorite eateries, where I can get the New York favorites that I can only savor once a year even though I'm in So. Carolina. Perhaps while the others are basking in the hot sun, I'll lose myself in various attempts at creating artwork masterpieces. It doesn't matter if they won't turn out exactly right or that I'll probably throw them away after returning home.

What matters is that my head will be clear; that I will have disconnected myself from the outside world. I will have a semblance of peace and relaxation. Is there anything that could be better than that?

The only downside to all my fun is that it only lasts one week! Saturday to Saturday, with a transition day on Sunday. Come Monday morning everything that I was able to postpone will come rushing back at me. This is just how the world works. There seems that there is no way to avoid this… or is there?

As we go through our service this morning…there are many instances where it seems that we are looking for something more than just peace and quiet from our normal, overbearing world. Before I began this message, I opened with "Grace and Peace to you, from God, our Father, and our Lord and Savior Jesus Christ." Next in the Kyrie we asked for peace on three different occasions. In the Canticle of Praise, we again asked for God's peace. Later on, I proclaim, "The Peace of the Lord be with you all" and finally in the blessing at the end, we ask that the Lord "look upon us with favor…and grant us Peace!"

When we get to the point in the service where we share the Lord's peace with each other, it's obvious that we don't wish ill will, sickness or misfortune to come upon our neighbor. We don't dismiss these possibilities but at this particular moment we are extending our fervent hope that something bigger, the "Peace of the Lord," will be with them always. This is the peace that we are ultimately searching for. It goes without saying that we are searching for something that we cannot obtain in this world by our own actions, and certainly not on our own merits. There has to be something bigger than ourselves at work here.

There was once an extensive survey, conducted by a reputable polling agency. Questionnaires were distributed to people of all ages and occupations. The key question was: "What are you looking for most in life?" Amazingly; when the answers were tabulated, the answers were quite different than what was expected. Answers pertaining to the accumulation of material goods were the expected answers, but in fact; the top three things that people wanted in life were instead; Love, Joy and Peace. This is quite interesting to say the least!

When things get overwhelming for me and I finally get it through my head that I can't solve my problems on my own, I realize that the only way to get the peace I desire is to pray to God about it. This isn't as easy as it seems. I, for one, have a hard time praying, as do many others (whether they admit it or not). This is especially true in a communal setting such as in church. There are too many distractions for me to concentrate. The woman in front of me is moving around. The gentlemen next to me is clearing his throat. No matter where I sit, the sun seems to shine directly in my eyes. Even if I have them tightly closed, it keeps me from focusing. It is then that I think back to what Jesus said about doing this out in the open where everyone can see you and where you play up to your vanity. Jesus said instead to seclude ourselves in our rooms and rid ourselves of all distractions and pray one-on-one with him. I do this in my room, but I take it one step further. I fold my hands in the conventional manner, but with a twist.

I have found that I can achieve the isolation I want by simply lightly pressing my thumbs onto my eyes. The result is a kaleidoscope of swirling colors; giving way to a blackness punctuated by star like specks and finally; an unfathomable black void that seems to me, like the immeasurable space between this earthly world and Heaven.

It is here that I can truly communicate with God. This is where I ask God to give me the strength to overcome the difficulties that are tormenting me. This is where I acknowledge my love for what Jesus has done for me and that I am quite unworthy of his love, in that he died on the cross just for us and absorbed all our sins. When I'm done with my petitions; I release the pressure and drift back to reality, feeling the peace, feeling the blessing that only Jesus can give.

Jesus makes a statement in John's Gospel that speaks directly to our troubled and aching hearts. He speaks to us about what we really want most. He tells us that we don't have to watch our lives fall to pieces. Jesus offers us the opportunity to enjoy his peace. Selfishly, we try instead to control our own lives, and find that we will have failed miserably.

The peace that Jesus offers is different from this world's peace. The world's peace is temporary and external. This peace is not found in meditation, drugs, material goods or achievements. It can only be found in Christ. It comes only to the true believers and to those willing to keep the faith. It is very possible that you are here today because you need something. There is something missing in your life. You see the world being taken over and that everyone is winning, and there is a feeling that you are losing control. That you can't handle all this by yourself. What you need is not something, but someone; and that person is Jesus.

The peace that we crave and the peace that Jesus offers is more than what we can obtain on our own, and only He can give it. It is something that is unique to him.

According to Martin Luther, "The conscience can never know peace when it is oppressed by sin." "Nor can it experience a joyful confidence in God." We need to abide in Jesus' Word and obey His commandments. This shows our love for Jesus and opens up the path to his kingdom.

In today's Gospel, we read that even though Jesus will no longer be with the disciples on Earth, He certainly doesn't leave them hanging. He sends the Holy Spirit to take his place. Jesus says to his disciples:

"But the Holy Spirit, who the Father sent in my name, will teach you all things and enable you to remember all that I have said to you." "The Holy Spirit will make all things understandable, so that you will experience the assurance that all will be as I have told you." "I have told you this before it occurs, so that when it does occur; you may believe."

We have been justified by faith. And because of this faith we have gained the ultimate peace of eternal life that only Christ can give. The trivialities of today's world will be dealt with. The onslaught of trials and temptations brought on by Satan cannot prevail. He will not win. Jesus says He must leave but will return again. The disciples, at this point in time, do not realize the implications of what Jesus is saying and Jesus knows this. To further comfort the disciples, He says: "My peace I leave with you; my peace I give to you." "I do not give to you as the world gives." Because this is still all new and confusing to the disciples, Jesus adds; "Do not let your hearts be troubled."

We have heard these words before, about eternal life and where Jesus is going, in my favorite verse which is also from John chapter 14. At the very beginning of this chapter, Jesus talks about his impending death and what it means for us when he says: "Do not let your hearts be troubled." "You believe in God; believe also in me." "In my Father's house there are many dwelling places." "If it were not so, would I have told you that I go to prepare a place for you?" "And if I go to prepare a place for you, I will come again; and I will take you unto myself, so that where I am, there you shall be also."

Jesus is leaving, as he is now relating to the disciples. By the way of the cross, He is going to the world beyond to prepare a place of peace for all of us. But He will be back! The world around us, as He says, will be left to the prince of this world, the devil. But Jesus leaves us the Holy Spirit in his place to help us keep the faith, and to keep his commandments, to love him and believe in him. If we do these things, the peace that surmounts all others will be ours.

There was recently a Facebook page that asked. "If you were to die tomorrow or get deathly ill, would the problems that seemed so important yesterday really matter anymore?" Jesus instructs us to step aside. Let the devil rule this world. Focus instead on the ultimate peace that we all deserve. The dwelling place that he goes now to prepare. There, we will gain the peace that transcends all others. The peace that only our Lord can give.

If we can learn to focus on the ultimate peace; if we can learn to leave the trivial annoyances behind – the unpaid bills, the appliance breakdowns, the vehicle repairs – then our vacations will be of a different nature. The week-long breaks will no longer exist or come to such an abrupt ending.

Our priorities will be forever changed, because of Jesus' sacrifice on the cross. Our newfound pleasures will have no end. The ultimate peace that we've been seeking all along will finally be ours, forever!

Thanks be to God!

Alan G. Vandewater
May 1, 2016

John 14: 23-29

23 Jesus answered him, "Those who love me will keep my word, and my father will love them, and we will come to them and make our home with them. 24 Whoever does not love me does not keep my words; and the word that you hear is not mine but is from the Father who sent me. 25 I have said these things to you while I am still with you. 26 But the Advocate, the Holy Spirit, whom the Father will send in my name, will teach you everything, and remind you of all that I have said to you. 27 Peace I leave with you; my peace I give to you. I do not give to you as the world gives. Do not let your hearts be troubled, and do not let them be afraid. 28 You heard me say to you, I am going away, and I am coming to you. If you loved me, you would rejoice that I am going to the Father, because the Father is greater than I. 29 And now I have told you this before it occurs, so that when it does occur, you may believe."

"The Beatitudes" (or "Be Attitudes")

Today's gospel reading is about the part of Jesus' "Sermon on the Mount" commonly known as the Beatitudes, as recorded by Matthew. Words so comforting in their own paradoxical way, that even non-believers have heard of them, and have used them in their own lives. Words which, no matter who translates them, originally came from the lips of our Lord and Savior Jesus Christ.

We are all familiar with either Luke's version or Matthew's; or we might even merge the two together in some way. But whose words do we believe? Maybe I shouldn't say that, for they are Jesus' words, but whose writings; whose translation; whose embellishments should we consider to be the gospel truth?

Today our focus is on Matthew's eight-point interpretation, as opposed to Luke's four-point version in which certain verses are also included in Matthew.

Luke is more noted as a storyteller, more of a revolutionary; whereas Matthew is more religiously bent, and more apt to speak in terms of Christology. Luke offers the standard introduction: "Blessed are the...and then states the direct opposite in a "woes" section. Matthew does his version with a totally different approach. He states the "Blessed" opening in all his lines, but then he follows immediately as to what the reward will be for the blessed person.

So why am I bringing up Luke so much when the reading for today is clearly from Matthew? Because the two are firmly entwined. There is a lot of debate in Bible circles as to who influenced whom; who copied whom; and just where did their sources come from? But this isn't the point. The two apostles' words will never be identical. It would be the same as if our other Lay Leader was preaching the same Gospel reading at the other church today, and me here. Our words are not going to be identical, but the theme – the message – will be the same and that is ultimately what is most important.

There is the misconception that Jesus was speaking to the crowds. Even though Luke and Matthew disagree on how Jesus spoke, they both point out the fact that Jesus taught the disciples first and did not direct anything to the crowds at that point. In Matthew's version, and because he is trying to persuade the people that Jesus is more than just another prophet, he relates, as we read, that

> "Jesus went up the mountain and after He sat down, his disciples came to him and then He began to speak to them and teach them, saying…"

This would be in a manner that we would more likely associate with a relationship between a king and his subjects. Luke describes it a different way. He says Jesus came down from the mountain, with the twelve, and stood at a level place, with a great crowd of his followers and a great number of people who wanted to be healed. Then in verse. 20 Luke says: "Then He looked up at his disciples and said…" But today the reading is about Matthew; so, let's look deeper into what his message reveals and its importance to us. The first segment reads:

#1. Verse 3 "Blessed are the poor (in spirit) for theirs is the kingdom of heaven."

Matthew's first beatitude differs from Luke's in that Matthew adds the words "in spirit" in his line. Whereas if you are poor, as Luke says, then yes, it sounds fair that you should be rewarded with the "kingdom of God;" but Matthew emphasizes "poor in spirit." This to me seems (at first) to take things in a whole different direction. If you are full of the Spirit, it would seem right and proper that you be rewarded. If you are deficient in the Spirit, well, that's just too bad; but here is where we might need to reorganize our first impressions.

If you are "poor in spirit" you are like a sponge. You are full of all kinds of empty nooks and crannies that have the capacity to absorb. You have ample room to soak up God's Word, and to heed the words that He sends to you. With this newfound humbleness, you have the capacity to understand your sinful place in the world, and the need to yield to His authority. You have the capacity to acknowledge the fact that everything you have...everything you are, everything you do, is only because of the grace of God. When you are humble and devoid of pride and selfishness, you are then willing and able to surrender to the authority of God and to live your life here on earth as he would like you to. Therefore, yours will be the kingdom of God.

#2. Verse 4 "Blessed are those who mourn...for they will be comforted."

Of course, we think first of the obvious, perhaps at the funeral home where we are most likely suffering the loss of someone who was close to us; someone that we loved dearly. Or it could be the loss of a pet, that was like one of the family, or it could even mean the deep, overwhelming sorrow you feel from a personal, impairing affliction. So, we ask...how can mourning be a blessing?

Referring back to our first "beatitude": when we are humble and realize that all our gifts and blessings come from God, then we mourn all the more for our sinful nature and the sins of the world. As it says in the Bible, "Jesus mourned over Jerusalem and for the world." When we look back and realize that mankind had it all in the Garden of Eden; that we were made in the image and likeness of God, and then we lost it all, forever…we mourn. The people who first heard this in our Gospel reading today, knew of their sinfulness; they could mourn their actions, but they had no idea of what was to transpire. They had no idea at that moment, that Jesus was to die on the cross for mankind's sinfulness. They had no idea that the comfort for their mourning, of which Jesus spoke, would entail such a high price. When we look at our "fallen nature" and that Jesus had to die because of us, His action on our behalf becomes a blessing. It then creates a desire within us to act within our abilities, to improve ourselves, to improve the world, and to do what is right by God…and therefore we will be comforted.

#3 Verse.5: "Blessed are the meek, for they will inherit the earth."

When we first think of "meek" we picture a whiny little guy, cowering in the corner, perhaps in a wrestling ring, and this big brute is moving in to finish him off. We can't help thinking one of two options. If this guy is so mousy, then why should he inherit the Earth? Wouldn't the stronger individual be more appropriate? Then we ask: possibly, maybe the timid, unassuming fellow has been battered and tormented for so long that he deserves to get something in the end?

The word for meek in Greek means…humble. A humble person is one who is gentle and kind, one who can display a docile spirit even in the face of adversity. A person who is humble is not the one who cowers timidly in the corner. Rather he is the one who displays great courage in his ability to exhibit enormous self-control amid hardship and overwhelming odds. We can see this when the meek person displays anger over someone who is being treated badly, but can somehow check his anger when he himself is the one being treated unfairly.

Meekness is moderation. Meekness is living a God-controlled life. Moses, Abraham, Paul, David and St. Stephen were meek people. We shouldn't see meekness as a detriment, but as an asset. Even Jesus was not the violent, overpowering warlord that the Jews had hoped to gain in the Messiah. Among our actions on earth, we need to remember to be meek in the face of the Lord. We need to learn not to resist his will, or his directives, but to be obedient in all things. This is something that doesn't seem to be a priority in today's world.

A meek person is one who has realized that happiness doesn't lie in possessions obtained, or worldly goods, or domination over someone else; but in a right relationship with God. When we get our priorities in order we will see for sure that the meek will indeed inherit the earth.

#4 Verse 6: "Blessed are those who hunger and thirst for righteousness, for they shall be satisfied."

The first three beatitudes were an emptying process, whereas now we come to seek answers for our helplessness. Taking from Greek translations once again, we learn that this verse from Matthew denotes one of desiring, not just a little, but all the righteousness of God.

When we are physically hungry, we find that we will stop at nothing until that deep-seated desire is satisfied. We will ruthlessly rummage through cabinets, shelves and even dumpsters, looking for that can of soup, those leftover crackers, or that bruised piece of fruit. We are so desiring, that all of our focus is on satisfying that need. Nothing stands in the way... Nothing else matters... Nothing else is as important.

This is the same type of focus we need to have in our search for righteousness. Righteousness cannot be achieved by our own strength. It can only be achieved by being right before

God. It is not obeyance of the law, which in itself leads to self-righteousness and our judging of others. It is a righteousness that is given to us by God, because we believe in Jesus Christ. We don't hunger and thirst after happiness, but after righteousness. Blessed is the man who hungers and thirsts for this righteousness; for he will be filled.

#5 Verse 7: "Blessed are the merciful... for they will receive mercy."

Justice is getting what we deserve. Mercy on the other hand is getting what we don't deserve. We say in the Lord's Prayer... "forgive us our trespasses, as we forgive those...who have trespassed against us."

Because we have received the mercy of God, through repentance, we ourselves should be merciful. We who have received forgiveness, can show forgiveness. The Greek word for "mercy" translates as "getting into the skin of." When we do this, we can more fully identify with a person's feelings. We can feel his pain; we can empathize with him. We can experience what he's going through. In the same way God was merciful to us. He felt our pain.

Through Jesus Christ, God came "into the skin" of man. As we can identify with our fellow man, if we are merciful, so did God "identify" with us. This beatitude is like a beacon of light, which shows us the way of self-examination. If we are merciful to others as God was to us.... then we will receive mercy."

#6. Verse 8: "Blessed are the pure in heart...for they will see God"

Moses, John and Paul all said that no one can see God here on Earth. But Jesus said that the "pure of heart" shall see God. To be pure of heart means to be free of all selfish intentions and self-seeking desires. This seems to be impossible, because as Paul reminded us, we all have sinned and fallen short of the glory of God. As an example, the Pharisees were concerned with outward appearances of righteousness, but God was more concerned with the workings of the inner heart. How many of us have performed that act of personal sacrifice, that act that was free of all self-serving desires and individual gain? I would venture to say, not many, because it requires an act of pure, unselfish love. Jesus comes to mind obviously; however, so do firefighters, soldiers, and police officers. As John says, "No greater love hath a man, than to lay down his life for another." What compels these people to put others first, often at great personal risk? What makes them see their actions as "a calling," rather than just a duty? Why do they often feel that Jesus is watching over them? Could it be the Holy Spirit at work? Could it be the renewed heart in the unrenewed body that fuels a saved Christian? Those whose lives are truly saved have been transformed by the grace of God. They are those.... "who shall see God."

#7. Verse 9: "Blessed are the peacemakers.... for they will be called children of God"

When we first picture a peacemaker, it's usually in the form of someone standing between two warring parties, their arms outstretched attempting to keep the two apart and thus unhurt. This might take the form of an innocent victim facing off against the schoolyard bully. It might mean a married couple so at odds with each other and so frustrated that it has erupted into a serious altercation. It could also mean, among other scenarios, two rival gangs seeking to control the other for prominence.

God first established peace between himself and man. The peacemaker strives to maintain this peace between God and man and also to bring peace and friendship to others.

Unfortunately, as long as the forces of evil prevail, sometimes there is no way to have peace except to destroy it. Even though peacemakers live peaceful lives, they cannot bring peace to others if they do not possess it themselves. The Lord wants them to be filled themselves first, with the blessings of peace, and then they can communicate that peace to those who have need of it. Peacemakers obtain this characteristic by being at peace with God, and then being transformed by the regenerating power of the gospel. It then becomes their desire to become God's ambassadors to a troubled world.

As peacemakers they need to go further in this world than simply stopping quarrels. They need to find ways to get mental assistance for the bully and his victim, so they understand their actions and consequences. They might need to provide counseling for the married couple, so they can work out their differences and resume normal lives. They might need to go as far as creating task force committees, so that the warring gangs can see that there are other alternatives besides power and prestige and material gain.

When peacemakers have obtained this blessing from God and then strive mightily to bring peace to the world, then, they will be called children of God."

#8. Verse 10: "Blessed are those who are persecuted for righteousness' sake, for theirs is the kingdom of heaven."

Jesus is very up front here in telling the disciples that they will be persecuted! It was happening right then, when the Christian movement was just getting off the ground. The four Jewish sects surrounding the new Christians were already set in their ways as to who Jesus was, and what should happen, and how. People generally react in very strong way towards something that is new to them or is contrary to what they accept as the norm, and this was no different. The Christians were the "new kids on the block."

Jesus taught in ways that were contrary to the accepted mannerisms. This upset the elite and caused consternation because they were challenged by Him. This was not the Law they were used to following. Being righteous, or Christlike, was not something they were used to (and neither are we), and that led to persecution. When we face persecution, it might not always be imminent danger or the loss of our lives, but the strain of trying to withstand the social temptations and the pressures of the world we live in. We tend to think, as we sit here contentedly, that this was all over in the few centuries after Christ. Not so, as we see when we pick up any daily newspaper. We are getting bombarded here in the US and Europe verbally and morally. People are being violently persecuted in the Middle East and Africa and elsewhere. It might seem as if all this is futile and unsuccessful and never ending. It will be never ending until all accept Christ's being. But had past Christians been unsuccessful, we would not be sitting here today.

In any respect, following Christ's directives and being right with God in spite of being persecuted will lead to rejoicing and great exultation. We will become God's children, which in turn will lead to a "great reward in heaven."

To sum up our lesson for today:

True happiness or blessing is found only in God's kingdom and in his righteousness, not in the supposed blessings of this world such as pleasure, wealth, achievement, or acceptance. We might think these things will satisfy us, but in the end only God can fulfill the longings found in our hearts and sate our natural desire for happiness. True happiness comes not from selfishness or striving for worldly goods or power, or achievement; it comes only by giving ourselves away and practicing the virtues of meekness, mercy, purity and peacemaking.

When we do these things, we become the kind of people Jesus intended us to be in the beatitudes. The kingdom of God, as we humbly acknowledged, cannot be obtained by force, birthright or achievement. It belongs only to those whose sole desire is to accept God's righteousness, live according to Jesus' words, and try in all their endeavors to imitate Him.

Thanks be to God!

Alan Vandewater
February 2, 2007

Luke 5: 1-12

1 When Jesus saw the crowds, he went up the mountain; and after he sat down, his disciples came to him. 2 Then he began to speak, and taught them saying: 3 "Blessed be the poor in spirit, for theirs is the kingdom of heaven." 4 "Blessed are those who mourn, for they will be comforted." 5 "Blessed are the meek, for they will inherit the earth." 6 "Blessed are those who hunger and thirst for righteousness, for they will be filled." 7 "Blessed are the merciful, for they will receive mercy." 8 "Blessed are the pure in heart, for they will see God." 9 "Blessed are the peacemakers, for they will be called children of God." 10 Blessed are those who are persecuted for righteousness' sake, for theirs is the kingdom of heaven." 11 "Blessed are you, when people revile you and persecute you and utter all kinds of evil against you falsely on my account." 12 Rejoice and be glad, for your reward is great in heaven, for in the same way they persecuted the prophets who were before you."

"The Saints and the Escalator"

We are already halfway through my favorite month, November, which includes Thanksgiving; Veteran's Day; my birthday; Election Day; and Martin Luther's Birthday. It all begins with All Saint's Day. I like All Saint's Day, as opposed to All Hallows' Eve or Halloween. Halloween scares me!

It scares me just as much as the stories from the Book of Daniel or Revelation, both of which speak of all kinds of monstrous creatures and all sorts of calamities and consequences, all described in what we call apocalyptic language. Thankfully; like all the books from J.R.R. Tolkien's Lord of the Rings trilogy and other such tomes, fanciful, sometimes frightening images turn eventually into a story where "good triumphs over evil".

I have a vision of "All Saints Day; a dream if you will, of all these nice people ascending to Heaven while the rest of us look on. In my dream, all these people are dressed like Robert Young in "Father Knows Best" or like June Cleaver in "Leave it to Beaver." (I think we can venture a guess as to how long I've been nurturing this scenario!) Along with these people are others dressed in white robes, but they can't be angels because they don't have wings.

In my dream, they're not ascending through the clouds to the great beyond by floating or going up a staircase; "Oh No! Instead, I envision them going up and up in a never-ending procession, on an escalator! I really don't know what happens next because in this dream, as in all my others, I wake up!

Knowing how escalators work, I'm not sure whether these kind people stepped off the end onto the highway to Heaven, or if they fell to that bottomless pit we call Hell. How can we be certain that we will step off this conveyance and not tumble downward like lemmings falling off the proverbial cliff? Our first reading today certainly doesn't allay my fears. It reads in part; *"But at that time your people shall be delivered, everyone who is found written in the book." "Many of those who sleep in the dust of the earth shall awake; some to everlasting life and some to shame and everlasting contempt."*

It's the escalator dream all over again. How can I be reassured?

We find the author of Hebrews writing to a new group of Jewish Christians who were being persecuted. He wanted to replace their fears with a new confidence. He wanted to instill in them that they could get to know God with a new intimacy, a new strength, a new relationship. This was a totally radical concept for them which had previously been unattainable to them.

Some background about this: In the Temple in Jerusalem there was an inner room called "The Most Holy Place" or "Holy of Holies." It was separated from the rest of the Temple by a huge curtain. No one, except the High Priest, was permitted to enter this room because God's presence was believed to be there in a special way. Even then, the High Priest could only enter that room on the "Day of Atonement" and only after performing many rituals of purification. Before entering the "Most Holy Place" the high priest would sprinkle the blood from an innocent sacrificial animal in many places. This was a symbolic attempt to cover as much "sin" as possible. After that, the priest was required to go through several rituals of washing with water. He was trying to "purify" himself as much as he was able; therefore, enabling him to enter into God's presence. After all this ritual and after spending time with God and praying; the priest emerged and declared to all the people who gathered on the temple grounds, that their sins were forgiven, and that they could now go home, clean and satisfied.

I wouldn't be satisfied! This to me is like watching the *Wizard of Oz*. After all the trials and tribulations that Dorothy and the rest go through, they find the "Great Wizard" to be a wee little man hiding behind an elaborate façade. He was cranking a large handle, which made everything seem much larger and ferocious than it really was. How do we know for sure that this isn't what happened at the Temple?

The rest of the lesson informs us that the high priest, no matter how many rituals he goes through, cannot take away sin. We are now told that we have another High Priest, who by giving Himself as a sacrifice, has perfected for all time those who have been sanctified. This is the new covenant that was made between the Lord and his people; that he would "put his laws in their hearts and write them on their minds." (and most importantly to us) "and I will remember their sins and their lawless deeds no more."

We believers can now confidently enter into God's presence because of Jesus. No longer is the Most Holy Place kept separate from believers, by a heavy curtain. Jesus' death opened the curtain to us once and for all.

Scripture tells us that at the moment that Jesus died on the cross; the Earth trembled and the curtain at the temple was torn completely in two. Since that moment, no longer would we have to rely on the ministrations of a human high priest. Now we can approach God directly, thanks to Jesus.

The writer of Hebrews also reminds us that our guilty hearts have been covered by Christ's innocent blood; so now God looks upon us with favor rather than wrath. It also says that because we've been washed with the purest of waters, we have been purified completely. The stain of sin has been washed away and is no longer a barrier between God and us, his children.

There are many people who struggle to draw near to God because they feel they don't really deserve to be in God's presence. We are reminded today that none of us deserve to be in God's presence; but we can be; because Jesus has made it possible to do so.

I suspect that there may have been times when you yourself doubted the profession you've made: the existence of God, and whether he still cares for you because of things that have happened. Or maybe people attack you because of your faith and try to undermine it.

In Mark's Gospel, Jesus warns us; "Beware of those that try to lead you astray." "Many will come in my name and say I am He." "And they will lead many astray." The remedy in these instances is to hold on to what you believe to be true. To seek God with your undivided loyalty. Now that we have been assured of our place in Heaven, the latter part of today's reading from Hebrews, encourages us to channel our efforts elsewhere. He challenges us to live lives that are marked by love and good deeds, and to help others attain those same goals. Unfortunately, that's easier said than done. If we really believe that Jesus has made it possible for us to approach God directly we should strive to live differently. We should be different than all the rest of the world.

When people hurt us, we should try to respond with love, rather than hatred. When we disagree with someone, we shouldn't seek to "win;" or to hoard it all for ourselves. We should try to act with good deeds and reach out to those who are hurting or ignored. We should care for others without seeing if "there's something in it for me." We should be the kind of people who live our lives to please God rather than ourselves. We should learn that our process of growing in faith is never over.

We cannot sit back and conclude that we've arrived. God is concerned about our journey and how we got there. He wants us to experience all that this life can offer; and He wants us to be dependent on each other.

This can only be achieved if we have a living and vibrant relationship with God. When we live according to His wishes, the last step off the escalator will certainly lead to Heaven and not the other way.

Thanks be to God!

Alan G. Vandewater
November 18, 2012

Hebrews 10: 19-25

19 Therefore, my friends, since we have confidence to enter the sanctuary by the blood of Jesus, 20 by the new and living way that he opened for us through the curtain (that is, by his flesh), 21 and since we have a great priest over the house of God, 22 let us approach with a true heart in full assurance of our faith, with our hearts sprinkled clean from an evil conscience and our bodies washed with pure water 23 let us hold fast to the confession of our hope without wavering, for he who has promised is faithful. 24 And let us consider how to provoke one another to love and good deeds, 25 not neglecting to meet together as is the habit of some, but encouraging one another, and all the more as you see the Day approaching.

"The Marriage"

You gentlemen who are married: I want you to think back to your wedding day. The day when, according to your wife, you would say the last two intelligent words she's ever going to hear you say. It's a sort of emotional day. On one hand you're bold and decisive. You've flirted, wooed and courted this woman, and now you're going to marry her. But it's also a day with just a little trepidation and concern. Even though you're supposed to do everything together, you can't help but to think of the ramifications of what the next hour will bring. You; as the husband, as the man of the house, will most likely be responsible for everything that may come up in the future.

Judeo-Christian law, from which our modern-day law stems, basically puts the ultimate legal responsibility for housing, support, education, debts incurred, etc., on the man. It's a huge undertaking. It requires some real thought on the part of the groom, as to what he's actually getting into. It would be so easy to turn to your entourage standing behind you; wave your arms and shoo them all out the side door, while declaring: "It's too much responsibility!" "It's too much for me!" "It's too overwhelming!" "I simply can't handle it!" It would be far better to escape now, while the going's good, even though more than a few people will be absolutely offended.

As it turned out, you didn't! You stood your ground resolutely. After her father kisses her goodbye, you join hands, you and your bride; and stand up before the altar together, in the spotlight, literally and perhaps figuratively. The minister is kind of a shadowy figure, along with the people in the congregation. The very people you agonized over; debating who would sit with whom; who would get along with the others; who you hoped wouldn't make a spectacle of themselves. All those folks are forgotten as you and the bride concentrate on the business at hand.

You are about to be united through your wedding vows to each other. You will no longer be two separate entities, but one unit melded together. Living together; working together; facing a future full of unknowns, and unseens.

There is a reason why we hear during the ceremony our promises to be together; "in sickness and in health," "for better or worse," "for richer or poorer," until death do us part. It's a huge undertaking that should not be taken lightly.

I've often heard of people who were married by the Justice of the Peace or by a city official lament the fact that they didn't have a church wedding. Even little girls and teens who fantasize about a lavish wedding with all the trimmings, want it held – where else? -- in a church. Why? What is the attraction? What is the common denominator? Could it be that we feel God's presence there? Could it be that we feel more reassured that we have God's blessing on the undertaking on which we're about to embark? Could it be that God, through the Holy Spirit, is surrounding you, guiding you, encouraging you with faith?

Notice that I used the word "faith" rather than the word "hope." "Hope" implies that things aren't so good now, and that maybe they'll get better later on. Faith, on the other hand, means that things are great now, will be better later, and will be solid as a rock at the end. Faith means not having any trepidations.

Even so, the minister continues with the service and then he asks each of the participants one final time; "Do you take this person, to be your lawfully wedded…" (blah, blah, blah). This is either the moment of commitment, until death do you part, or the last final chance to escape.

Today's gospel reading from John is very similar to the scenario I've just described. It is in fact a wedding; a marriage. Jesus has just finished feeding and teaching the mass of people. He then decides to confront them with what we call "the hard saying." Jesus tells the crowd that they must believe and "eat of my flesh and drink of my blood" in order to gain eternal life. This is too much for the majority of the people in attendance to understand. They can't accept it. They don't believe it. They can't go through with it. They run out the side door, so to speak.

We say to ourselves, "What was the matter with them?" "Why couldn't they believe?" "Why couldn't they make a commitment?" It's so easy for us to make that assumption; but remember this is the very first century. They are living in the moment. They haven't yet seen Jesus crucified, dead and buried. They haven't yet seen him resurrected. They haven't yet seen Jesus come back to earth after his Ascension. This is made all the worse by the fact that the people see Jesus mostly as just the son of the carpenter Joseph and the son of Joseph's wife, Mary.

We've been told about how our lives change based upon our decisions. Today's first lesson tells us that the time has come for the people surrounding Joshua to make their decisions. Do they want to serve the gods of their ancestors, leaving us; and escape through the side door? Or do they want to dedicate their lives to the one true God? This is a wedding day of sorts. The people needed to make a decision about which way they'll go. Joshua declares his commitment by saying, "As for me and my household, we will serve the Lord." After hearing Joshua say this, the people rallied and recounted all the good things that God had done for them. They also affirmed their commitment by saying: "Therefore we also will serve the Lord, for He is our God!"

We learn also that there are always evil forces around us. Forces working to influence us into making wrong decisions, to misplace our priorities, to make us turn away from God and the things we know to be right. In the Bible we are admonished to "take the shield of faith, with which you will be able to defend yourself from all the arrows of the evil one." "Take along also, the helmet of salvation and the sword of the spirit, which is the word of God."

All these observations have one thing in common: faith. Faith enables us to face the things we do not know, the things we cannot see, the trials and the tribulations. To face the future without trepidation. To make a firm commitment. Peter and the other remaining disciples are willing to make this ultimate commitment. Faith is not hoping God can; it is basing your actions on knowing without doubt that He can!

As we read more from John's Gospel, we find that there is a wedding of unusual proportions about to take place. The spotlight and focus are now on this. The people are now the "Bridegrooms" and Jesus is the "Bride!" This is an event where through the actions of the Holy Spirit, and with God's blessing, a union will take place unlike any other. The people feel God's presence surrounding them; encouraging them; comforting them. They are making choices that will significantly affect their lives and like Joshua; they are not concerned about what the others might think or believe. The bride and the bridegroom will become united as one. They will no longer be separate entities, but one unit. Melded together; working and living together; where from this day forward they will abide wholly in Jesus and he in them. In spite of this, the disciples know that things will have the potential to be more "poorer than richer," more "sickness than in health," and probably much "worse before they get better" – infinitely better. In spite of this, this is not yet a done deal. Jesus knows who will believe, and even the one who will betray him. Like the minister who married us, Jesus asks one more time, testing them, giving them one last chance to change their minds, "to escape."

"Do you also want to go away?" Jesus asks. Peter then replies for himself and for the others: "Why should we bother to think what others believe?" "Why would we seek answers from them?" "We have come to believe that you are the Son of the living God." "You have the words of eternal life!"

Why would we mortals, like the disciples; want to go anywhere else?

Thanks be to God!

Alan G. Vandewater
August 29, 2012

John 6: 51-69

51 "I am the living bread that came down from heaven. Whoever eats of this bread will live forever; and the bread that I will give for the life of the world, is my flesh." 52 The Jews then disputed among themselves, saying, "How can this man give us his flesh to eat?"53 So Jesus said to them, "Very truly, I tell you unless you eat the flesh of the Son of Man and drink his blood, you have no life in you. 54 Those who eat my flesh and drink my blood have eternal life and I will raise them up on the last day; 55 for my flesh is the true food and my blood is true drink. 56 Those who eat my flesh and drink my blood, abide in me and I in them. 57 Just as the living Father sent me, and I live because of the Father, so whoever eats me will live because of me. 58 This is the bread that came down from heaven, not like that which your ancestors ate,

and they died. But the one who eats this bread will live forever." 59 He said these things while he was teaching at Capernaum. 60 When many of his disciples heard it, they said, "This teaching is difficult; who can accept it?" 61 But Jesus, being aware that his disciples were complaining about it, said to them, "Does this offend you? 62 Then what if you were to see the Son of Man ascending to where he was before? 63 It is the Spirit that gives life; the flesh is useless. The words that I have spoken to you are spirit and life. 64 But among you are some who do not believe." For Jesus knew from the first who were the ones who did not believe and who was the one that would betray him. 65 And he said, "For this reason I have told you that no one can come to me unless it is granted by the Father." 66 Because of this many of his disciples turned back and no longer went with him. 67 So Jesus asked the twelve, "Do you also wish to go away?" 68 Simon Peter answered him, "Lord, to whom can we go? You have the words of eternal life. 69 We have come to believe and know that you are the Holy One of God."

"Love One Another, As I Have Loved You"

A Happy Mother's Day to all of you out there that claim the designation of "mother" in any way. We appreciate everything that you do and have done for us.

There are two things every man learns sometime in his life and they are: There is no wrath like a woman's, and there is no tighter bond than between a mother and her children. A good illustration of a mother's love is changing a baby's messy diaper over and over, whereas a father will do it once and proclaim, "never again!"

Today's Gospel lesson is about "love" and especially about us and our love for our neighbors. Jesus says in the opening verse; "As the Father has loved me, so have I loved you; abide in my love." But then Jesus adds the stipulation that all of us seem to have trouble with: "If you keep my commandments, you will abide in my love, just as I have kept my Father's commandments and abide in His love." This already gives us enough to think about, but then Jesus takes it one step further and is very specific. He says: "This is my commandment; that you love one another as I have loved you." Keeping God's commandments is not something at which we particularly excel.

As you have undoubtedly heard by now, the news dominating the headlines in recent days has been the rioting and mass destruction in Baltimore, Maryland. (I'm not going to get into reasons or finger pointing or blame, but I am simply using this incident to bring today's lesson from Jesus into modern terms.)

One bright spot, if you want to call it that, in this whole fiasco is some TV footage that went viral and spread across the globe. It was on Facebook, Snapchat, Instagram, You Tube and every media source available. It showed a video of a mom chasing her older child home. She was wailing away at him and when he tried to outdistance her, she then caught up with him and wailed away again and again. This was the release and sheer outpouring of her pent-up emotions. Another notable aspect of this encounter is that the woman was reportedly wearing a bright yellow top, white pants and was carrying a bright pink cellphone! There is no way that anyone was going to miss seeing her.

It seems this woman was in her apartment and was watching the news on TV and spotted her son, clad in a mask, throwing stones and cavorting around with the rest of this out-of-control frenzied crowd. Somehow, and I mean somehow, she goes into this chaotic scene and finds her son. How she found him in this flood of people I'll never know. I can't even find my wife in a Wal-Mart store! She then starts teaching him a lesson he'll never forget, while the video cameras catch it all. Right away she's an instant celebrity! Everyone is tweeting and posting comments like "Hooray for Mom." "Parenting as it should be." "Mom for Mayor," as the current Mayor wasn't exactly handling this riotous situation very well.

When interviewed later, she said she did it out of fear. Not fear of the crowds or fear of herself getting hurt; but fear for her son, the fear of him getting injured or even worse.

In verse 13, Jesus says: "No one has greater love than this; than to lay down his life for one's friends." Jesus, of course, is talking about Himself and is relating this final message to his disciples. But we need to remember that we are also His disciples. We know that this woman, overcome by love for her son, could have been seriously hurt or even killed for doing what she did.

But there were others there who exemplified Jesus' love for us. What first comes to mind are the firefighters, the police and the soldiers. Fellow men and women who put their lives ahead of themselves – for those they didn't even know, let alone their friends. Giving of yourself is hard, especially when it might lead to death, and is not something that comes naturally to many people. But there are many for whom it is just something they do without regrets. Sadly, there are times when the unthinkable happens and we hear ourselves listening to that verse once again, where Jesus reminds us "to love your neighbor as I have loved you."

Christian love revolves around two loves: the love of God and the love of each other. The fact that we struggle with this shows that we are only human. It seems that we find ourselves in a position where we feel we can do one or the other, but not both. But loving others is exactly what God is calling us to be actively doing. To experience the type of love that requires giving rather than receiving. We see here in Baltimore, here in America that we have fellow citizens bringing all manner of harm to innocent neighbors for a perceived injustice. People doing such revolting, despicable acts, that we simply can't understand why. We cannot comprehend. We shake our heads in despair.

We adamantly voice our opinions and make our feelings known. We say in no uncertain terms that we consider these acts totally out of sense with our righteous values. Here is where we are in conflict with ourselves. We don't give these rioters the five-star rating that we gave the mom. Regardless, Jesus says that these are our neighbors too, and that we should love them as ourselves and as He has loved us!

Let's ponder this dilemma that we find ourselves in. We know deep down that these are fellow human beings, just like us. We wonder "what happened?" "What can we do?" "What should we do?" We know for sure that at one time they were innocent babies, pure and straight from their mothers' wombs. We surmise, almost certainly, that as toddlers they were most likely very pleasant young children. But somewhere along the line someone changed them; someone influenced them, or even hurt them in some way so that this riotous melee ended up being the only way they could react. To get revenge. To heal their hurts.

We know that Jesus wants us to love them too, but it seems we just can't. In my sense of values, honorable, righteous people like the mother get tops in my five-star rating system. People like the rioters and others of the same ilk, fare much lower. I cannot love all others as I love myself. I don't have it in me to expand my love to that level; or do I?

Even though the devil and others would try to convince me that this is perfectly all right, Jesus doesn't make a list of exemptions. I can't conveniently scan my list to see if there's a way I can rationally get out of this. There is one way around this dilemma and that is to stay connected to the source of love, and that source is God. He will be the source of all my needs, much like the baby that is connected to his mother for all his needs after being born. This connection, both motherly and godly, cannot be broken. We can be nurturing to all in our lives.

A good example of this is a soaker hose. A soaker hose is nothing but an inert, dry length of rubber. Like us it also has a lot of holes. By itself it doesn't serve any useful purpose. For it to be effective it needs to be to be connected to a source of water. When it gets connected to water source a huge transformation occurs. Water not only flows into it, but also through it and out of it! It then not only receives the water itself, but now it passes the water onto whatever is around it. The more we increase the pressure, the further it reaches. The more seeds it lands on, the more growth it enables. And so, it is for us to love Jesus, and for us to love as He has loved. Like the hose connected to the water source, we need to be connected to God. When we are connected to Him, His love not only flows in us; it flows through us, out of us and onto to those around us. The more we increase the pressure the more people it reaches, the more seeds of hope it lands on. The more seeds that are watered, the more good we can do. Between God's help and those around us we find that we can do what we thought we couldn't do on our own. We thought we couldn't love our neighbors as we love ourselves. We thought they were despicable. We assumed that they didn't share our values. We surmised that they were beyond hope. We thought they were so much different from ourselves that we could not possibly love them.

We need to know when to ask for God's help and to trust in His love for us. In verse 11, Jesus says; "I have said these things to you, so that my joy may be in you, and that your joy may be complete." Just like the mother from Baltimore who kept her son from harm, by doing whatever was necessary, even with the possibility of death looming close, Jesus kept us from the wrath of God by dying on the cross. By that action He treated us like one of his children, where the bonds of love could never be stronger, nor broken. This is very much like a mother whose love for her children is impossible to break.

Do as Jesus commands. Love your neighbor as He has loved us.

Thanks be to God!

Alan Vandewater
May 10, 2015

John 15: 9-17

9 As the Father has loved me, so have I loved you; abide in my love. 10 If you keep my commandments, you will abide in my love, just as I have kept my Father's commandments and abide in his love. 11 I have said these things to you so that my joy may be in you, and that your joy may be complete. 12"This is my commandment, that you love one another as I have loved you. 13 No one has greater love than this, to lay down one's life for one's friends. 14 You are my friends if you do what I command you. 15 I do not call you servants any longer, because the servant does not know what the master is doing; but I have called you friends, because I have made known to you everything that I have heard from my Father. 16 You did not choose me, but I chose you. And I appointed you to go and bear fruit that will last, so that the Father will give you whatever you ask in my name. 17 I am giving you these commands so that you may love one another."

"Hallmark and the Gospel"

I like Hallmark movies. Not because they have a lot of redeeming value, but because, unlike drama series, they don't require any special, mind draining effort on my part to understand. The plots are simple and very predictable.

In the beginning everyone starts out happy. Then a problem arises. Everyone continues to search for an answer as the plot thickens and time runs short. Then a "knight in shining armor" arrives to save the day, and then everyone lives happily ever after. You could almost doze off in the middle of the movie and upon awakening a short time later, would still be able to grasp the story and see the ending.

I watched one such movie this past Christmas. The plot was going according to plan, as always, but somehow the time sequence seemed out of sync. I said to myself, "Something's not right here. It's not going to end the way it usually does." Sure enough, it stopped and the screen said, "to be continued." I wasn't very happy and grumbled a bit, but I figured "Oh well; it'll be on tomorrow or maybe next week." Imagine my surprise when they announced; "to be continued... CHRISTMAS 2016!" I believe I let out some rather "unchurchly" words at this revelation. Really? Who's going to remember the beginning; or make the connection when the two dates and segments are so far apart?

Luke's Gospel today is very much like this. Its main point refers back to Isaiah 61 verses 1 & 2, where we learn that the Jewish people have just been released from captivity after being held by the Babylonians. They then found their Temple in Jerusalem and their homesteads in ruins. They tried to rebuild, but things weren't going very well. The people were getting very discouraged. They thought God had abandoned them. The times were hard; food was scarce; hope was in short supply. They were in so much mourning at this point that they took to wearing sackcloth, and they put ashes on their foreheads to illustrate their deep anguish. All was looking dismal. Then behold; along comes the prophet Isaiah who says to them: "God is here." "He will deliver." "He will save." "He will make you a mighty nation." "Through you; God will keep his promise to bring salvation to the world."

It seems as if our movie plot is following true to form in this scenario. There is hope. Then the movie stops abruptly, and we're left hanging. We don't know if the problem will ever be resolved. We don't know if our "knight in shining armor" will arrive, or whether all is lost, and happiness will be permanently out of our reach.

This isn't the way movies are supposed to end. There has to be a part two; a conclusion; a happy ending. Maybe that will change someday.

Let's fast-forward to the Gospel reading from Luke. Luke 4:14 begins by telling us that Jesus has returned to Galilee and is entering Nazareth where he was raised. In John 2 we saw Jesus in a social context, as he was concerned about his mother and the wedding in Cana. This was where Jesus performed the miracle of turning the water into wine. Jesus enjoyed the days he spent with his family and the social scene; but now he is entering Nazareth to attend the synagogue as was his habit. We are told: "news about him spread throughout the whole countryside." "He taught in their synagogues and everyone praised him."

I know from my own experience as a former worker in a synagogue that these places of worship are special in their own right. There is a quiet peacefulness, a tangible aura of dignity, of learning, of God's presence within. They don't have the crowds, the hustle and bustle, or high priests. They don't follow the sacrifices that the Temple would require. Synagogues have no priests or preachers, but they do have Rabbis. Every man has an opportunity to participate in a time of reading and learning. Men would volunteer to read a passage from the scrolls of the Old Testament signified by their standing up; and afterwards, they would sit down and were then expected to explain to the congregation what it meant to them. The Amish tradition is very similar to this. This is the kind of atmosphere into which Jesus is entering this day.

Jesus stands up and is handed the scrolls. We don't know if this was the reading for the day or divine providence, but Jesus stops when he gets to the words of Isaiah and begins to read: "The Spirit of the Lord is upon Me, because He has anointed Me to bring good news to the poor." "He has sent Me to proclaim release to the captives and recovery of sight to the blind, to let the oppressed go free." "To proclaim the year of the Lord's favor." This was a favorite reading of the Jewish people because it was a passage of hope, a passage of deliverance. It reminded them that God was still with them, no matter what was to come. Jesus returns the scroll to the attendant and sits back down.

All eyes and ears are upon Him, because they know that He will now explain the passage to them. Jesus speaks; and when He does, He really grabs their attention. The very first line is the one that shocks the participants. Jesus says: "Today the Scripture has been fulfilled in your hearing." What He is saying is that in that little synagogue, He had fulfilled the scripture reading, in person, right in front of their eyes.

That on that day he announced that He is God's salvation to the world. God's deliverance. God's promise of hope to the world. God's promise of freedom.

Jesus is claiming in this moment to be the one that Isaiah was pointing to long, long ago; He is our movie's "knight in shining armor." Is this going to be our movie's "happy ending?" Let's look further and see what this means for us.

Jesus is going beyond what Isaiah has said. Jesus didn't mean that only one nation would be restored. He didn't mean that the physical Temple would be rebuilt. What Jesus was talking about was a spiritual restoration, not a physical one. Jesus was talking about God's plan of salvation for the whole earth; not just the nation of Israel. In this synagogue full of questioning faces, Jesus was saying that through Him, God would grant salvation to all people. That salvation would come to us even today, and forevermore.

Part of that salvation is for us to preach the Good News. The news that God is with us, that He cares for us. There is forgiveness; there is hope; there is renewal. These are the exact same things Isaiah was talking about ages before. Jesus knew even then, when He made this announcement, that the world we live in today would be what it is. A place where violence and bad news would be commonplace. Where we would witness man's inhumanity to others on a daily basis. Where we live among all this hatred and violence. A place where it seems that sin is ever rampant, and that death and the devil are alive and well. It would seem only logical that we too, like the Israelites, would at some point begin to wonder if God was still around. We would begin to feel just as they felt after the Babylonians invaded: hopeless, fearful and uncertain in our faith.

Admit it. Haven't we all wondered this even just a little bit? Maybe a lot? Where is God among all this chaos and grief and troubling times? Perhaps we need to be reminded, above all, that God has not abandoned us. That amidst all the troubles in the world, our God is still here. This is our hope; this is our deliverance; this is our good news. The fact is that the good news of salvation through Jesus Christ still needs to be proclaimed "loud and clear," especially now!

Jesus also says in this passage that He was sent to "proclaim release to the captives; the recovery of sight to the blind; to let the oppressed go free." Isaiah was talking about those still in Babylonian captivity; but Jesus goes way beyond that. Jesus is talking about the release of the peoples of this world from our sin and our own selfishness, because of His death upon the cross.

Jesus released us from our captivity to ourselves, which is really the basis of sin. He awakened us to our own mortality and reminded us that only He can set us free. Jesus speaks to those who are oppressed because of disease, or lack of food, shelter or clothing. He speaks to those who are oppressed because of race, creed, or other factors.

Jesus' act of salvation freed us from the oppressions of this world. Today the Scripture has been fulfilled in our hearing. Our knight in shining armor has come; and is here. The "good news" is present now, today, with us! This seems like the way the movie should end. It certainly seems like a happy Hallmark ending to me!

Thanks be to God!

Alan Vandewater
January 24, 2016

Luke 4: 14-21

14 Then Jesus, filled with the power of the Spirit, returned to Galilee, and a report about him spread through all the surrounding country. 15 He began to teach in their synagogues and was praised by everyone. 16 When he came to Nazareth, where he had been brought up, he went to the synagogue on the sabbath day, as was his custom. He stood up to read. 17 and the scroll of the prophet Isaiah was given to him. He unrolled the scroll and found the place where it was written: 18 The Spirit of the Lord is upon me, because he has anointed me to bring good news to the poor. He has sent me to proclaim release to the captives and recovery of sight to the blind, to let the oppressed go free, 19 to proclaim the year of the Lord's favor." 20 And he rolled up the scroll, gave it back to the attendant, and sat down. The eyes of all in the synagogue were upon him. 21 Then he began to say to them, "Today this scripture has been fulfilled in your hearing."

"The Wedding at Cana"

The Gospel of John has been characterized by preachers, students and theologians alike as being one of the hardest Gospels to interpret; and I am certainly not going to be the last to join their ranks. The other three Gospels are somewhat similar. They are written in such a way that it's easier to dissect them and go off on tangents regarding morals, sinfulness and a whole slew of other analogies.

For example, I could easily talk about marriages, drinking habits, joy, etc. but that's not where I'm going today. John is different. He thinks differently; he writes differently; he sees things differently. If this were to be a group of high schoolers and our evangelists were part of the group, John would be the geek or the nerd. He would be the one who expressed himself in such a way that the others might not take him seriously. He would be labeled "the kooky one." John, in his writings, gets the most mileage out of "symbolism." When reading his Gospel; we would do well to "read between the lines."

Our reading for today is about the wedding at Cana and the issue of Jesus changing water into wine. In this modern age; the fact that they ran out of wine doesn't impact us fully. All we have to do is simply make arrangements to go out and purchase enough to make it through the event, and everything will be "hunky dory." That is not so in this case! A little background.

No one speaks ill about the water in the Middle East. It is scarce and conservation efforts are high, but we shouldn't assume that its scarcity has been replaced by consuming vast quantities of wine. Not so! There were many poor people involved in the production of wine and it was a cash crop for them. It was pretty much the same as me trying to get the same quality of filet mignon that I was used to in NYC, in a restaurant around here. Producers aren't going to consume their best product themselves, when the market and the profits are better somewhere else; unless it is a very special occasion! And so it was in this case. The daily normal fare for these people would be cheeses, olive oil, breads and water. However, the occasion of a wedding changes things drastically.

The couple's parents would have scrimped and saved for a very long time to make sure that they did this wedding right. It was a step in the right direction to have a menu consisting of sheep, calves and every fine delicacy they could muster. And of course, the freely flowing wine! Family and friends passed high judgment on those who could not carry off a wedding in high style. You can see in these origins here, some of our modern-day concerns regarding the quality of weddings and especially the receptions. Now you can see the importance of Mary's statement to Jesus and her implied hint that He needs to, and can, do something about the situation at hand.

Once again, we are surprised at one of Jesus' retorts. "Woman, why do you involve me?" "My time has not yet come!" Perhaps Mary, who certainly knew of the circumstances regarding Jesus' life, figured that upon his delayed return – especially with the disciples in tow – "Now is the time…He should declare himself openly." Jesus of course knew that His time was in the hands of the Father and wouldn't let himself be manipulated, even by his own mother. Mary accepts this apparent indicator of Jesus' new perspective of himself, and directs the servants to "do whatever He tells you." "Do whatever He tells you" is also a reference for us, as Jesus' servants, to put our lives in Christ and to acknowledge his power and to follow His commandments!

Still, regardless of what He said, Jesus has no desire to allow this lack of wine to affect the joy of the wedding, nor to bring extreme embarrassment to the hosts. Instead He uses this as a teachable moment. This is the first of Jesus' many signs and as we see further on in his ministry, these signs are usually a portent of bigger and better things to come.

At the wedding site, there are six rather large jars that Jesus has commanded to be filled with water. Then He quietly turns the water into wine, without laying hands on them, or praying to the Father, or waving a wand over them or saying magic words. "He simply wills it; and it is done!" Don't get misled; I'm not talking exclusively about the wine or its quantity here; my main emphasis at this point is on how it is achieved. He wills it! This gives us a whole new slant on things. Take for instance our words in the Lord's Prayer: "Thy kingdom come...Thy will be done." We could look at this in one sense, that if God wills it to be done, then it is up to us to try to do it one way or another, and follow his commandments. Or we can look at this in another light. If God wills it to be done; then it can and will be done because God chooses it and not because we had anything to do with it! The one who can do things like this, in a manner like this, is nothing less than God himself.

The water; as we said beforehand is scarce and sacred, and is adequate, but wine is better. Water symbolizes Jesus as the essence of life; but now the new wine is the "good wine," "the best of the best." Jesus then relates; "If you then who are evil, can give good things to your children; how much more will your Father in Heaven, give good gifts to those who ask Him?" We remember this in our Eucharist, where we recall Jesus' last words to his disciples at the Last Supper. He takes the cup and says to them: "Drink, all of you. This is the new covenant, in my blood, shed for you and for all peoples, for the forgiveness of sin."

Just as Jesus supplied the best wine at the end of the wedding, in abundant quantities as a sign, it is also a sign to us that He wants also to supply us with the "good wine." We will never lose thirst because we have received His grace in abundant quantities, because of his redeeming sacrifice on the cross.

One more bit of symbolism here, which regards the number and the purpose of the jars themselves. These large-capacity jars that the Jewish people used for purification, were empty. Jesus, Himself talks about the "blindness" of the Jewish people, especially the leaders. The empty jars and the lack of wine speak of the emptiness of their religion at the time of Jesus' appearance. Think ahead to Jesus' trial and crucifixion and the aforementioned dislike of Jesus by the Judeans, and others, who didn't believe. These are the people who have need of the good wine and the promises of Jesus.

In another symbolism; in the Jewish tradition seven is the number that symbolizes "completeness." We notice in our reading that there were only six jars available to be filled with the new, good wine. Therefore, we can conclude that Jesus is communicating that all is not finished yet. That "His hour has not yet come." But it will come and be completed as we well know.

It is comforting to know that the same power of will that Jesus used that day is still being executed with us, His believing people. We don't have to see Him. We don't have to touch Him. We don't have to mutter "magic words." We simply have to believe! If we believe in His will; we are as safe and well provided for as if he were here beside us.

A wedding changes things. A greater marriage feast than the one at Cana will be held someday, when Christ himself will be bride and we the believers will be the bridegrooms. Blessed will be those believers who will be called to the marriage feast of the Lamb.

At this feast you won't have to worry about running out of anything. The food will be more satisfying than anything you've ever had before, and you will never be thirsty. This will not be a be a get-together that will only last a week, but one that will last a lifetime.

Yes; John can be confusing, the symbolism overwhelming. But if you read "between the lines" you will see that Jesus was not just concerned about making wine for the wedding, so that the host wouldn't look bad; He was concerned about pointing them, and us, in the right direction, to the source of Life. The very best life of all. So, as we found out today in these few eloquent verses, this wasn't just another simple wedding.

Thanks be to God!

Alan G. Vandewater
January 17, 2010

John 2: 1-11

1 On the third day there was a wedding in Cana of Galilee, and the mother of Jesus was there. 2 Jesus and his disciples had also been invited to the wedding 3 When the wine gave out, the mother of Jesus said to him, "They have no wine."4 And Jesus said to her, "Woman, what concern is that to you and to me? My hour has not yet come." 5 His mother said to the servants "Do whatever he tells you." 6 Now standing there were six stone water jars for the Jewish rites of purification, each holding twenty or thirty gallons. 7 Jesus said to them "Fill

the jars with water." And they filled them up to the brim. 8 He said to them, "Now draw some out, and take it to the chief steward." So, they took it. 9 When the steward had tasted the water that had become wine and did not know where it came from (though the servants who had drawn the water knew), the steward called the bridegroom 10 and said to him, "Everyone serves the good wine first, and the inferior wine after the guests have become drunk. But you have kept the good wine until now. 11 Jesus did this, the first of his signs, in Cana of Galilee, and revealed his glory; and his disciples believed in him.

"The End Times and Our Decisions"

I'm not ready for the change of seasons. After last winter's prolonged snowfall, and being cooped up in the house for weeks on end, I couldn't get enough of summer. I basked in the sun as much as I could. I even had a chance to "get away" for a whole week for a beachside vacation, but soon it was over. I couldn't stay longer, doing what I really wanted to do. I had responsibilities and obligations to take care of. Labor Day came and went, then Election Day, and now here I am preaching my first Advent message ever, just three days after Thanksgiving! Where did the time go?

Everyone's thoughts for the next four weeks will dwell on Christmas: the partying, the fun, the traditions. The sheer magnitude of all the material gifts we might receive. The good times to be had. We dream of feeling good after a few eggnogs and a full belly, which causes us to fall asleep, literally and figuratively. The gift-giving frenzy to come which was started simply by the three Magi. They knew the importance of their journey; and then they traveled a long distance bearing three gifts of things that were precious to them, to present to the Christ child.

Here we are today, focusing on Jesus' first coming, with joy and celebration. Then here I come reciting Mark's Gospel, telling of gloom and doom and his warning to "stay awake, keep alert." Let's be honest. We spend a lot more time celebrating all the tangent events surrounding Jesus' coming, than we do the actual sobering event which started it all. We might spend an hour or two in church, and then it's back to the festivities. And when it comes to celebrating Jesus' Second

Coming; which was the reason for the first, we pay even less attention.

Jesus says the Second Coming will catch us by surprise. As Mark relates, "The sun will be darkened, and the moon will not give its light; and the stars will be falling down from Heaven, and the powers in the heavens will be shaken." "Then they will see the Son of Man coming in the clouds with great power and glory." "Then He will send out his Angels and gather his elect from the four winds; from the ends of the earth to the ends of Heaven."

Similarly; from Luke 2, verses 25 and 26 we read Jesus' words: "There will be signs in the heavenly bodies and distress among nations." "People will faint from fear and foreboding of what is coming upon the world, for the powers of the heavens will be shaken." In Matthew; Chapter 24 verse 3, we read of the disciple's concern when they ask Jesus; "Tell us; when will this be and what will be the signs of your coming and the end of the age." In verse 8 Jesus (in essence) replies: "There will be wars and rumors of wars; nations will rise against nations and kingdom against kingdom and there will be famines and earthquakes…this is just the beginnings of the birth pangs…do not be led astray."

Just about a month ago there was an urgent post on Facebook, about how the Sun will be darkened for three days shortly before Christmas. NASA supposedly confirmed that this will be true due to some cosmic dust blocking the Sun's rays. Imagine the logic and the consequence of no light or heat from the Sun for three days! And you thought last year's Polar Vortex was bad? I don't even want to think about this possibility. It was later surmised that this was a hoax; but what if it wasn't?

Would we be one step closer to what Jesus had predicted? Jesus said: "Only the Father knows the day and the hour of the end time." I wonder how many people believed enough in this seemingly real post, to take stock of their lives? To maybe take things more seriously, and change the direction they were heading? Too many of us (as Jesus warns) use our time trying to figure out the odds of when the Second Coming might be. Meanwhile we "keep an eye on the signs," attempting to figure out how much time we have to party, to acquire material goods (like Christmas presents), and to rise as high as we can in status.

We are very much like a college student, who at the beginning of his term was given a syllabus by his professor. In it was listed everything that would be required and when it needed to be done. Even so, the student chose to ignore it; then suddenly the day comes when everything is due and there is absolutely no way the student can get it done in time. People spend their whole lives trying to figure out when they will finally need to "get right with God." Some plead on their deathbeds, when they, like the college student, realize that they've run out of time.

"Why do we do this?" "What are we afraid of?" We spend more time celebrating Jesus' first coming than we do His second. We know what the first coming meant and its necessity and we are glad; but then we revert to our own selfish desires once again. For some reason we are afraid of the second coming.

We avoid this topic and instead, content ourselves here on Earth with amassing material goods and attempting to figure out what the odds are; so that we can "enjoy" them to the maximum.

When we lose someone close to us, we mourn, we grieve. We listen numbly to people who try to console us with words like; "He's in a better place." "He's no longer suffering or in pain." "It was his time." or "Jesus reached out His hand, and he took it." We listen to our clergy relate the story of Jesus and Lazarus. We hear my favorite words from John 14 verse 2, which reads: "In my Father's house there are many dwelling places." "If it were not so would I have told you, that I go to prepare a place for you." "And if I go and prepare a place for you; I will come again and take you unto myself, so that where I am, there you may be also."

We know, as Jesus said, that we are on this earth for only a short time and then we will be with Him. So why do we still exert all our energies and spend all our time doing foolish things, instead of focusing on our faith and the things Jesus has promised us? We spend all this time celebrating and contemplating His first coming. We then ignore, as best we can, His Second Coming. It should be more of a celebration than it is. We should be looking forward to God's promises and hoping that the Second Coming will come to us quickly; that it happens soon. That we will be ready instead of unprepared when God deems the hour and the day and takes us home. Instead we focus on how much time we have left to "do our own thing." It's ironic that when we put Him aside, so we "can enjoy life," we find that we separate ourselves further from the very one who is the source of the true life we so desperately crave.

As we continue living here in the present, we must remember that we are living now, to live again! Jesus is reminding us that we must not allow the joys of the present, or the things of this world, to distract us from our real purpose of living. The real purpose is to "Glorify the Lord and to enjoy Him forever." We must always remember that the best way to enjoy "right now" is to keep our eyes focused always on the one who is leading us, to another time and another place.

Don't be led astray. Don't put Him aside.
Be watchful. Be alert. Be awake

Thanks be to God!

Alan G. Vandewater
November 30th, 2014

Mark 13: 24-37

24 But in those days, after that suffering, the sun will be darkened, and the moon will not give its light, 25 and the stars will be falling from heaven, and the powers in the heavens will be shaken. 26 Then they will see the Son of Man coming in the clouds with great power and glory. 27 Then he will send out the angels and gather his elect from the four winds, from the ends of the earth to the ends of heaven. 28 "From the fig tree learn its lesson: as soon as its branch becomes tender and puts forth it's leaves, you know that summer is near. 29 So also, when you see these things taking place, you know that he is near, at the very gates. 30 Truly I tell you, this generation will not pass away until all these things have taken place. 31 Heaven and earth will pass away, but my words will not pass away. 32 "But about the day and the hour no one knows, neither the angels in heaven, nor the Son, but only the Father. 33 Beware, keep alert; for you do not know when the time will come. 34 It is like a man going on a journey, when he leaves home and puts his slaves in charge, each with his work, and commands the doorkeeper to be on the watch. 35 Therefore, keep awake--- for you do not know when the master of the house will come, in the evening, or at midnight, or at cockcrow, or at dawn, 36 or else he may find you asleep when he comes suddenly. 37 And what I say to you I say to all: Keep awake."

"You Reap What You Sow"

I have a reputation for not being a morning person. I'm the one all the disparaging "morning person" remarks are about on Facebook. My favorite time is the end of the day when I'm ready for bed once again. This is my most relaxing time. The day is done. The TV is off, the jammies are on, my glasses are removed, my hearing aids are out. My glass of iced tea is on the nightstand; and now, it's just me and the magical world of reading.

I generally have three classes of reading materials, which for simplicity today I'll call: fiction, nonfiction, and educational. "Fiction" is my favorite when tired at bedtime. It requires no real thought. You can almost sense what the author is going to say next. You have a good idea of how the plot is going to evolve. It's enjoyable reading. After that we have nonfiction. These readings involve a little more thought. You might have multiple characters to keep track of; or even two or more parallel stories to pay attention to. I try to stay away from these whenever possible. Lastly, we have my "educational" category. I avoid these like the plague! These are the books that require the most thought. Sometimes you need to read the lines, over and over again, before you think that you're getting just a glimmer of what the author is trying to express. This is certainly too trying to grasp, especially at bedtime.

Our Gospel reading for today from John, is very much like my last category. Of the four Gospels, Luke is the easiest to read. It is free flowing; it's poetic; it's "easy to digest" reading. This is my so called "fiction." Matthew and Mark come next. They frequently copied off each other, so we are familiar with a lot of their stories. They are in my so-called "nonfiction" category. Their accounts are a little harder to decipher; but not so much so that it taxes our brains. We can handle these…if we pay attention.

But then along comes John. John's Gospel is squarely in my "educational" category! What he writes often doesn't make immediate sense. His words are complex and can be confusing. Many a time we find that his words don't mean what we initially thought them to mean. We find the need to read verses over and over before we get that glimmer of understanding. A lot of times it can be full of "opposites" and "contradictions," and very much confusing.

Verse 20 of today's reading relates to us that there were Greeks (gentiles) who wanted to "see Jesus." They had come to the Passover feast; which would imply to us, that they were God-fearing men. They approach Phillip (an apostle) seeking favor. This is because Phillip was a Greek and from Bethsaida, which was more in line with the Greek culture. The men could've wanted to meet with Jesus for any number of reasons. This throws Phillip off as being contradictory to the situation at hand in dealing with these "gentiles." He seeks out the disciple Andrew for more input, and together the two of them decide to place the gentiles' request directly to Jesus. Jesus' answer, as we read in verses 23-26, seems to have nothing to do with this request. Jesus says all the "opposite" things. Things that are confusing. Things that we can't seem to make sense of.

"The hour has come for the Son of Man to be glorified."

"unless the kernel falls to the ground and dies…it remains a single seed." "But if it dies… it produces much fruit."

"Those who love their life will lose it." "and those who hate their life… in this world, will keep it for eternal life."

"Whoever serves me must follow me, and where I am, there will my servant be also."

Pretty confusing stuff, wouldn't you say? Then Jesus gives us some "good news." "Whoever serves me...the Father will honor." Jesus, in typical fashion, is pointing us to the future. Pointing to something that is greater. Jesus is living beyond the moment and He knows exactly why He is where He is. His mission is clear in his mind. He knows what He must do. Did Jesus know this was the time? As in his birth, when the "gentiles" from afar visited him on that first Christmas, signaling the beginning, was this request from the gentiles "to see Him," a signal that his purpose to be "a light to all nations" was certainly at hand.?

This whole scenario occurred in the days after Jesus' triumphal entry into Jerusalem; riding on a colt, surrounded by the exulting, thunderous adulation from the crowds around him. In spite of all this; Jesus wasn't distracted at all. He was focused completely on the mission to come.

When we read John's accounting of Jesus' words, can we see how this might apply in our own lives? Do we find ourselves unfocused and out of control? Do we have so many things going on, so many responsibilities, so many unmet expectations that we can't focus? Are we so busy living for the moment, that unlike Jesus, we cannot see beyond today? You will find that you are not the only one.

People who are spiritual aren't exempt either. Right at this moment I feel overwhelmed by a Synod class that I need to take. The amount of reading I need to do; the essays I need to write. I'll have to be honest with myself. When I hear about "living for the Glory of God" it sounds a little uncool, a little boring. It feels like I have to be some sort of religious clone.

That I need to be against anything that is "enjoyable" in my life. That isn't something that I want to readily embrace.

I framed a church bulletin once that I enjoy immensely; but I find it hard to do as it says. It reads, "You shall love the Lord your God, with all your heart; with all your soul; and with all your mind; and you shall love your neighbor as yourself." I mean well, but I have a hard time actually doing what it admonishes me to do. I fall victim to my own wants, my own selfishness, my own lack of control. Though I try not to, I find myself falling into the same habits of those around me. I try instead to make a name for myself; amass as much stuff as I can, to pad my resume and achieve my successes. I want to do all the "enjoyable" things in life, before it's too late. I forget (conveniently) that my goal in life should be to honor and love the Lord, and to live in accordance with His truth. I should not see "obedience to God" as a hindrance to life, but as a doorway to Life!

Our living for the moment has its repercussions. For instance: when we were younger, our parents may have cautioned us to save some of our money for a rainy day. That our willingness to do without now would bring a greater reward later. If we did without candy now, it might mean we could get a bicycle later. If we resisted that shiny new toy now, maybe we could get a car later. If we made do with what we had now, and saved for a down payment, we just might be able to afford a nice house later.

This is what Jesus is trying to point out. Doing without now is an investment in the future. We have to be careful of the lure, which is taking the easy way out. In our Scripture lesson today, Jesus refers to a kernel of grain to exemplify this point. Taking this kernel, we could serve our inherent desires by storing it and then selling it on the market. Or we might grind it up and eat it. Or we could invest it by planting these kernels in fertile soil and wait for the future harvest, which would benefit us more in the long run.

It's no different with our human lives. We can consume our lives in our present "gratification" mode that seems so prevalent now, or we can devote our lives to the Lord with the confidence of a future harvest. If we focus on ourselves, we spend our time in the present, in the "right now" frame of mind. Our time and efforts end with us right now, in the present. It is like the seed that is eaten. There is no future. However; if you take the other route, which is living for others (like being a part of a Christmas "Angel Tree" project) your life becomes abundant. Your interests are widened. Your desire for life is increased. Your life has more meaning. As Jesus said: "He who loves his life, shall lose it…and he who hates his life in this world shall keep it unto life eternal." If you consume your life now, enjoying it along the way, then you can't have it later. If you devote your life to others and give yourself up to God's disposal for the greater good, then you will keep your life later on in Heaven. Jesus finishes up this long discourse of confusing directives by saying: "Whoever serves Me must follow Me, and where I am; there will My servant be also."

This works two ways. The way I understand it, we are promised that we will be with Jesus, in Heaven. It also says that we must not leave Jesus when it's convenient for us; that we must stay by his side wherever that may lead us. "Taking up our cross" is not just bearing burdens, but the willingness to follow Jesus even to our deaths. Think of those who have been slaughtered throughout the ages and even right now around the globe, because they choose to follow Jesus. To deny ourselves means that we do what God wants us to do, even if it's not the most convenient option. It calls for us to sacrifice the things we want and enjoy. We seek to understand, that by sacrificing now, we will enjoy the rewards later.

Do we strive to "see" Jesus as the gentiles did on two occasions, or are we content rather to feed our own selfish ambitions? Do we live in the "here and now" or do we focus on the future? Do we use our seed for ourselves or for the greater good? There is no promise that following the way of Jesus will be easy. We have only the promise that it will be worth it in the end.

Sometimes we need to take the harder road. To read the educational book, even though we'd rather not. To absorb the message even though we need to read it over and over to understand its intent. We need to put our faith in the future and not on what we can "see" now. Jesus looked to the future and made his choice for the greater good of mankind. What will our choice be?

Thanks be to God!

Alan Vandewater
March 22, 2015

John 12: 20-33

20 Now among those who went up to worship at the festival were some Greeks. 21 They came to Philip, who was from Bethsaida in Galilee, and said to him, "Sir, we wish to see Jesus." 22 Philip went and told Andrew; then Andrew and Philip went and told Jesus. 23 Jesus answered them, "The hour has come for the Son of man to be glorified. 24 Very truly, I tell you, unless a grain of wheat falls into the earth and dies, it remains just a single grain; but if it dies, it bears much fruit. 25 Those who love their life lose it, and those who hate their life in this

world will keep it for eternal life. 26 Whoever serves me must follow me, and where I am, there will my servant be also. Whoever serves me, the Father will honor." 27 "Now my soul is troubled. And what should I say--- Father, save me from this hour? No, it is for this reason that I have come to this hour. 28 Father; glorify your name." Then a voice came from heaven, "I have glorified it, and I will glorify it again." 29 The crowd standing there heard it and said that it was thunder. Others said, "An angel has spoken to him." 30 Jesus answered, "This voice has come for your sake, not for mine."31 Now is the judgement of this world; now the ruler of this world will be driven out. 32 And I, when I am lifted up from the earth, will draw all people to myself." 33 He said this to indicate the kind of death he was to die.

"By Whose Authority?"

Another pastor (from this congregation) and I were both of similar likes, having worked together as Fire Investigators here in Ohio, but also both volunteering as firefighters in New York. He was "upstate" while I was "downstate;" (actually about 20 miles east of NYC) on Long Island. For a while I had my own business, and it allowed me to do what I really wanted to do, which was to fight fires as much as possible. This wasn't very good for my business but great for me! As a result, I found myself responding whenever the whistle blew; from various firehouses and on whichever apparatus I was nearest to, when the alarm came in. Often times because of lack of manpower and the fact that I wasn't a driver, I found myself being the Officer in Charge. It was my duty to size up the situation upon arrival and direct in or turn back other responding apparatus. I also had to plan for whatever other resources I would need to accomplish the mission. I then relayed to the dispatcher what I wanted him to broadcast on the radio. Being as I wasn't a Chief, I had to give the authority as being from whichever unit number I happened to be riding on at the time.

Sometimes this was confusing to the dispatcher; in that the voice he was hearing didn't match whom he was used to hearing. Even though he was required to relay just what he was told, he would feel more confident if he could get it straight in his head just who was doing the authorizing. Even if he did recognize my voice, I'm sure he wondered why it wasn't whom he was used to hearing. Why was I on another apparatus instead of my own; and also, could my expertise and training be relied upon? We can sympathize with his feelings. When we read of a controversial story in the newspaper or on our tablets, we want to know its source. Is it reliable? Is it the view of a high-ranking government official with status, or just some guy in a coffee shop stating his opinion?

The scenario we read about in today's Gospel lesson comes during Jesus' last days in Jerusalem, not too long before His crucifixion. This episode follows right on the heels of Jesus' "cleansing of the Temple" where He knocks over the money changers' tables and announces that the people are profaning God's house.

As usual Jesus is at odds with those who supposedly held authority. These are firstly the Sadducees: a collection of the current High Priest, former high priests, and those who were supposedly on a good track to be high priests in the future. These people were primarily involved in anything having to do with Temple. Second in line were the Pharisees and Scribes, who today would be most likely classified as theologians. They were the religious experts who carried out the customs and the laws as they interpreted them. Lastly, we have the elders, a makeup of the most prominent families of Israel. All these groups had representatives in a group we call collectively "The Sanhedrin," the ruling body of the Jewish people.

So, you can see that Jesus was dealing with a formidable bunch of people. In a way, these men felt threatened. They felt angry and frightened. They thought, like my dispatcher or some other officers, that I was somehow usurping their hard-earned positions. This group considered themselves royalty, who were now being challenged by this lowly being and his band of ragtag disciples. It seemed that every time they attempted to "rein in" Jesus, they ended up being made to look ridiculous and even more inept instead. This had happened too many times before and now their tempers were boiling over. They were looking for any way possible to arrest Jesus and get him out of their hair and regain their authority. It seems that every question they leveled at Jesus was like a dual edged sword, delivered with an accusatory tone, and each time Jesus turns the tables back on themselves.

In today's Gospel, verse 23, we read their latest attempt to "trap" Jesus. They ask Him the question: "By what authority are you doing these things?" "And who gave you this authority?" I'm sure that when the Jewish leaders asked Jesus this question they anticipated that he would say: "I speak on my own authority," thereby giving them the opening they needed. They could then ridicule Jesus in front of the crowds and cast him out as a blasphemer. They weren't interested in gaining knowledge or insight; they were seeking the full impact of an accusatory question. Jesus retaliates quid pro quo, with a question of his own.

Jesus says; "I will also ask you one question." "If you tell me the answer, then I will also tell you by what authority I do these things." The question being presented to the elders was: "Did the baptism of John come from Heaven, or was it of human origin?" Seeing no easy way out of this predicament the elders talked quietly amongst themselves before finally declaring surprisingly: "We do not know."

John the Baptist, as you might remember, was a "boat rocker." He made waves. Maybe this is where our popular phrase "Don't rock the boat" originated. We read about him being an eccentric who lived in the desert and wore camel clothes and subsisted on practically nothing. He called on the people to repent of their sins and to be baptized. But more importantly, John pointed to Jesus as "the one to come." In other words; Jesus was the one who was "sent from God." John merely pointed the way, whereas Jesus is the Way.

Jesus' question to his accusers about John was difficult for two reasons. They couldn't say that John did not speak with God's authority because then they would be at odds with the general population. The people believed John was a prophet. Aside from making the accusers look foolish once again, it could very well get them stoned to death. On the other hand, if they said John did speak with God's authority, then Jesus would ask them why they didn't believe John's words and what John had predicted. So, the elite group pleaded with the equivalent of what today would be called "pleading the Fifth," the right not to incriminate oneself, by saying that "they didn't know." With the leader's refusal to answer, Jesus reverts back to his earlier terms and conditions. In verse 27 He says; "Neither will I tell you by what authority I am doing these things." As always, we are amazed at how skillfully Jesus, again and again, defers questions back to his accusers with questions of his own.

But there is another lesson to be learned here. We need to recognize the importance of Jesus' question. Who is Jesus? and by what authority does he speak is a vitally important question. "Is the Bible, (which we hold so dear;) "the word of the Lord, inspired by God" or is it just another popular religious text?" There are people out there who would disagree about the status of the Bible. If Jesus was just a wise man with great insights, then it is up to us (or the Sanhedrin in this case) to discern and interpret those insights about the things that he taught. If we do this, we wrongly become the final authority. We end up being the ultimate authority to decide what should be obeyed or disobeyed. On the other hand, if Jesus is God (as John proclaimed) then everything Jesus declared has, and does have, divine authority. We never did have vetoing power over Jesus' teachings. If; as we acknowledge, the Bible is from God, given to us by men through the ages, then it carries with it the binding authority of God. What He says is true. What He requires, we must do. Where He leads is where we must follow. Evidence points to Jesus as being the one universally sent by God, and the Bible as the "Word of God."

Another question arises about ourselves. Are we like the leaders in Jesus' time? Would we rather run away from something that doesn't please us? Or are we willing, instead, to embrace and concede to the evidence that is Jesus? Do we resist the truth because we don't like what it is saying; or do we swallow our pride and conceit, and submit to the authority of the one who knows us better than we know ourselves?

We cannot claim to be followers of Christ if we make accusatory questions and find the need to huddle together to discern answers. We cannot be the Christians Jesus wants us to be, if we need to ask the question, "By whose authority?" Jesus has already settled that question, long, long, ago!

Thanks be to God!

Alan G. Vandewater
September 28, 2014

Matthew 21: 23-27

23 When he entered the temple, the chief priests and the elders of the people came to see him as he was teaching and said: "By what authority are you doing these things, and who gave you this authority?" 24 Jesus said to them, "I will also ask you one question; if you tell me the answer, then I will also tell you by what authority I do these things." 25 "Did the baptism of John come from heaven, or was it of human origin?" And they argued with one another, "If we say, from heaven, he will say to us, "Why then did you not believe him?" 26 But if we say, "of human origin" we are afraid of the crowd; for all regard John as a prophet." 27 So they answered Jesus, "We do not know." And he said to them, "Neither will I tell you by what authority I am doing these things."

"Conflicts of Interest"

Every Christmas there is a battle. Should manger scenes be allowed on courthouse or public property? Can children sing Christmas carols in their school programs? Stores find themselves unsure whether to advertise "Christmas" specials or "Holiday" specials. People can't even agree on how to greet each other. In the sixties, some of these concerns stemmed from issues arising out of respect for those who didn't celebrate Christmas, namely our Jewish neighbors who celebrated Hanukkah; and then after 1966, the addition of Kwanza, an ethnic celebration created by and for African Americans, which seemed to contain some elements from both the Jewish and Christian celebrations.

When I was in grade school and later junior high especially, we had a sizable Jewish student population. We did call our concerts Winter or Holiday concerts, but we sang both Jewish songs and Christmas carols. Later on, "political correctness" got these religious tributes reduced to such secular songs as "Frosty the Snowman" and "Jingle Bells." We never had a problem with salutations either. If my Jewish friends were celebrating Hanukkah, I said "Happy Hanukkah." If it was Yom Kippur, I said "Happy Holiday." They in turn wished me a "Merry Christmas" or a "Happy Easter." No problems at all. The opposition that we face now is not coming from our Jewish or African American friends but from those who want to eliminate Christianity from every aspect of our public and private lives. There are people everywhere who hate Christianity!

In our Gospel lesson this morning from John we learn that this isn't anything new! People have been turning their backs on the real message of Christmas ever since Jesus first came down to Earth. In verses 9-11, we read: "The true light, which enlightens everyone, was coming into the world." "He was in the world, and the world came into being through him; yet the world did not know him." "He came to what was his own, and his own people did not receive Him." We are told that the true Light has come into the world. We are told that Jesus was the initiator; the one who started it all, because he wanted everyone to know the true light. He came because he wanted us to see and to know God, and to understand the purpose for which we were created. He came to bring us life.

So, the question is: Since Jesus is the one who is initiating our relationship and since he is doing it for our own good, rather than to harm us; we ask, what kind of people would reject him? John tells us of two groups of people. He tells us; "Though Jesus was in the world and the world was made through Him; the world did not recognize Him." Jesus made the world but when he came to Earth; the people ignored Him. It wasn't just the rest of the world who ignored Him; a greater insult was the fact that the Jewish people, God's chosen people; pretty much ignored Jesus. "He came unto his own...but his own did not receive Him."

Think of how absurd this is. It would be the same as if Jesus sat right here in these pews with us and we didn't pay attention to him. We didn't think he knew what he was talking about! The one whom we claim to worship, would be rejected. What is even more bewildering is the fact that the Jewish people had spent their whole lives waiting for a Messiah. Their ceremonies pointed to Him; their prayers longed for Him; but then when He arrived, they rejected Him.

Let's look into why He was rejected, or even better, why people of today also reject Jesus. The Jewish people were looking for a Messiah who would be a conquering king. They were looking for a victorious warrior; someone who would call them into battle, someone who would reward them. Instead, they got someone who was a humble servant, someone who called on them to be servants. They got someone who, instead of rewarding them, asked them to serve and to repent of their sins. This same thing happens today. People want a savior who will make all their problems disappear. Someone who will tell them everything is great. They have their priorities completely backwards. They want someone to serve them, rather than being called to serve. People want Jesus to be who they want Him to be. This is like some marriages, where one spouse or the other is convinced they can change the other person into who they want him or her to be.

People reject Christ, especially today, because he is deemed politically incorrect! Jesus came to this world bearing and telling the truth the way it has to be. We don't particularly like this, and some people can't bear it at all! Jesus doesn't excuse our sin by creating "spin." He doesn't mislabel our sin by calling it a disease, or tolerate us blaming our sin on others. He doesn't excuse our sins because we say that society has changed now, and things are different. Jesus doesn't do this. He condemns all of our sinful behavior regardless of cause. Jesus challenges us to take responsibility for our own lives and our own actions.

Jesus tells us we need to change, to admit the truth and to repent. As you can imagine, this doesn't play well in our society. We all have skeletons in our closets. The dark parts of our lives and character that we don't want others to see or discover. Jesus' light exposes that darkness. Most people don't want to face the truth of their sins. They want to pretend all is fine; so, they create stories and perform adverse actions to make sure all stays hidden.

Jesus tells us that we cannot save ourselves. He talks about the prevailing religion of today; the "I can do it all by myself faith."

In the time of Jesus, the Jewish people followed the philosophy that they would be saved if they lived good enough lives. They believed that if they kept the rituals; and tried to do good things, that they would receive God's blessing, favor, and ultimately eternal life. This is the way many people view it even today. Every other religion tells people that they can get to Heaven, Nirvana, or Paradise because of the good deeds they must do. In the case of Islam this could be the act of terrorism. They feel they must do this. They feel that if they follow all the rules they will be saved and go to their reward.

People might feel they are good when they are compared to other people. However, when they are compared to God's standards, they find that they are woefully inept and nowhere near what they should be. By God's standards, no one is righteous, not even one; and that there is no way to Heaven aside from God's grace. Jesus approaches this just a little differently. He says that in order to be a follower of Christ we need to realize that we are totally helpless to save ourselves. We need to go through Him. This goes against our grain. We don't like admitting that we've done wrong. We don't like submitting to God's will. We want to be God. Jesus told all those who would listen that the only people who will be right with God are those who put their faith and trust in the work of Jesus on their behalf and listen to the truth.

When I go to the doctor, I want him to tell me the truth. I don't want him to tell me that everything's fine, when it's not. I want to know the truth, so I can address it. In the infamous exchange in the movie A Few Good Men, Tom Cruise says; "I want to know the truth!" Jack Nicholson famously shouts back: "You can't handle the truth!" Jesus tells us the truth, and a lot of times we can't handle it. Jesus draws a line and says that those on one side of the line are right with God, the ones on the other side; are not. If you do not acknowledge Jesus as God, and that He is the only one who can save you, then you are not a true Christian and guess what: you're not going to heaven.

In Luke 21, Jesus warns his disciples; "All men will hate you...because of me." In John 17, Jesus talks to the Father and says: "I have given them your word and the world hates them." So, we shouldn't be surprised when people hate us and try to take the Christ out of Christmas and out of our lives.

We have two choices in this matter. Do we want to be politically correct or to be faithful? If our goal in life is to be politically correct and popular, then at some point along the way we will find, that we will have to compromise the gospel in one form or another. If we choose to be faithful, then there might come times (especially in this current climate) where we will be forced to take a stand. It's so much easier to follow a watered-down version of Christianity. One where we don't have to trust or obey. One where we never have to sacrifice or serve. One where we can excuse our sinful ways and rebelliousness by calling it "political correctness" and because it's deemed to be socially acceptable. We subscribe to a version where we are trusting in our own goodness and relying on our own resources to get us to Heaven. If so, you have been led astray by the very people that Jesus warned us about.

So, do not act as the world did long ago, or even today, but see Jesus for who He really is. See that He is your only hope, that He is the only one. Admit to Jesus your shortcomings and your sinfulness and ask for his forgiveness and acknowledge that he is the only way to Heaven. This is what separates us from those who don't believe. The unbelievers are quite intent that we true Christians change our ways and bow to their wishes. We need to stand firm in our faith and not make concessions to please the rest of the world. We need to escape the darkness and come to the light. Jesus is the light. He came into the world on that night so long ago for a reason; and we the faithful are that reason!

Thanks be to God!

Alan G. Vandewater
January 3, 2016

John 1: 1-17

1 In the beginning was the word, and the word was with God, and the word was God. 2 He was in the beginning with God. 3 All things came into being through him, and without him not one thing came into being. What has come into being 4 in him was life, and the life was the light of all people. 5 The light shines in the darkness, and the darkness did not overcome it. 6 There was a man sent from God whose name was John. 7 He came as a witness to testify to the light, so that all might believe through him. 8 He himself was not the light, but he came to testify to the light. 9 The true light which enlightened everyone, was coming into the world. 10 He was in the world, and the world came into being through him; yet the world did not know him. 11 He came to what was his own, and his own people did not accept him. 12 But to all who received him, who believed in his name, he gave power to become the children of God, 13 who were born, not of the blood or will of the flesh or of the will of man, but of God. 14 And the word became flesh and lived among us, and we have seen his glory, the glory as of a father's only son, full of grace and truth. 15 (John testified to him and cried out, "This was he of whom I said, "He who comes after me ranks ahead of me because he was before me.") 16 From his fulness we have all received, grace upon grace. 17 The law indeed was given through Moses; grace and truth came through Jesus Christ. 18 No one has ever seen God. It is God the only son, who is close to the Father's heart, who has made him known.

"The Disabled Woman"

There have been a lot of articles, editorials and opinion pieces lately about people who use the blue or red handicapped cards on their vehicles to gain parking spots closer to where they are going. This was created to make people's lives a little easier in coping with their disabilities. Now we hear of arguments from both sides about the need or lack of need, and maybe misuse. I'm not so naive to think that there aren't some people who might have needed this card once, found it convenient, and simply continued to use them, knowing a good thing when they saw it.

The situation only gets worse when an already disconcerted person witnesses the user of the placard seemingly having no trouble getting to the building's entrance. Looks can be deceiving and an onlooker cannot possibly make a determination as to whether this particular person is genuinely in need and is simply having one of his better days, or isn't worthy of having this special privilege in the first place. This observation takes in only the physical aspect, and that the person's mental state cannot even begin to be ascertained.

I have determined that there are basically four types of people who may surround a handicapped person. There are those who try to help too much, thereby "smothering" the person. Or you may have those who make it a point to complain loudly as they are doing their "good deed," so much in fact, that the needy person simply declares that he wants to go home and that the others can go merrily on their way without him. The third type wants to help, but isn't sure how, and a lot of times, ends up doing the wrong thing at the wrong time. The fourth remaining type are those who can only see what's in it for them, or how they've been offended in some way and see things through a form of "tunnel vision." We see a similar form of tunnel vision when churches host "Bikers' Weeks" and invite biker groups to one of their services as an act of inclusion. Automatically, when people see motorcycles and their riders, they assume the worst. They immediately make a judgment call, regardless of what they know for sure.

Not only is it hard to calculate a handicapped person's physical ability; there's no way we can fathom the mental anguish that these people are going through. As you saw in my description of the four types of people, the disabled person is beset by a whole host of problems, aside from his infirmity. These factors can lead to loneliness, isolation, frustration, despair, loss of self-worth, depression, and oftentimes sometimes lead to suicidal thoughts. This is when the disabled person becomes so weary of his situation that he pleads to the Lord to either make him some semblance of his former self; or take him to heaven where there is no more pain or suffering.

Fortunately, for a lot of disadvantaged people, there is more than a little shred of faith. They have the acceptance that there is an unknown reason for all their misfortune and that they possess more than their share of individual independence. This compels them to carry on and do their best, in spite of their current circumstances. This is most certainly true of the woman in our Gospel reading from Luke.

Luke tells us that Jesus is visiting a neighboring synagogue; and as a prominent visiting rabbi, he is conducting the Sabbath service. All is normal until He spies the crippled woman who is also attending services. Reflecting on the faith and independence aspect, note in the passage that the woman did not go to Jesus.

Unlike the other people who looked for favors or miracles, she didn't follow Jesus around from town to town. She didn't wail and cry out or grasp his robes for attention. She didn't beg or plead for any kind of special treatment. Jesus really could see her, physically and mentally. He knew what was going on in her mind. He knew of the isolation, the loneliness, the despair. He knew the frustration of trying to fit in socially with folks who don't always know what to do. Or perhaps they do the wrong things, or even don't do anything at all because of all the extra effort involved.

It seems that this woman had suffered for many, many years with a disease that fused her spine into a rigid; unbendable mass. This condition forced her to look constantly down at the ground, which made communication and awareness nearly impossible, without great effort on the parts of both parties. Her muscles were weak and atrophied. Also (as has been my experience) her brain was forced to spend half its efforts on keeping her body upright and safe and the other remaining half trying to focus on the task at hand.

Jesus saw her as a person worthy of his time! He placed His hands on her, and immediately her back was straightened. Her atrophied muscles become firm again. Her brain was once again able to focus on something besides simple survival. After eighteen long years, she no longer suffered pain and humiliation. The woman who was resigned to live faithfully and independently, in spite of her disability, was now set free to live a life without that crippling disease. Her mind was once again able to focus on the good things in life, and unlike the others we've read about, she immediately used this newfound freedom to praise God! What a cause for celebration! You would think that everyone around her would be happy for her.

This was not the case! The leaders of the synagogue were not happy. In fact; they were incensed! Even though it was not her fault, the woman was the prime reason the services had been disrupted, and in all probability, would not continue. They rebuked her, saying: "There are six days for work, so come on those days to be healed, and not on the Sabbath!" Here, in the midst of a great miracle, this synagogue leader feels the need to bring up a man-made law about work on the Sabbath! It's kind of like the disconcerted person in the parking lot that we mentioned earlier.

The leaders saw a law. Jesus saw the person. Jesus even goes so far as to call the leaders hypocrites! Oftentimes man-made laws serve a purpose, and generally they serve the greater good, but sometimes they can be inconsistent. Jesus seeks to point out this inconsistency by asking two questions. From verse 15, we read; "Does not each of you on the Sabbath, untie his ass or oxen from the manger and lead it to water?" The next verse asks; "and should not this woman, a daughter of Abraham, whom Satan bound for eighteen long years, also be set free from this bondage on the Sabbath day?" The Sabbath law was a good one. It was employed to serve as a guideline to keep people on track, to remind them to honor God especially on that day. But the leaders seem to be missing the point. In their zeal to honor God, they were inadvertently offending Him by sticking rigidly to the rules. Jesus instead, was putting the emphasis on how to honor God by healing and showing compassion for the disabled woman.

The leader's approach was negative, while Jesus' was positive! In spite of their laws, the leaders then realized it was okay to show compassion, as in giving their animals basic care. They also realized that they had failed God by not also showing compassion to the disabled woman, a child of God, whether it was the Sabbath Day or not!

Going back to our example in the situation with the handicapped space in the parking lot. When we get caught up in "tunnel vision" all we can see are our needs, our desires, our rules, and our perspectives. When using this process, we find that we throw compassion to the wind!

So, whether you are at the temple or the modern parking lot, remember to rejoice in the positive rather than the negative. Instead of lamenting the fact negatively, that you can't get closer to the store, rejoice positively that through the grace of God you are able to walk the extra thirty feet without much effort at all. Be thankful that you aren't inhibited in some way like a handicapped placard holder or the disabled woman, that Jesus healed.

Honor God, as Jesus did, by wishing the best to those who do not have and cannot do. Reach out positively instead of spouting the laws that may not apply in every case.

The kingdom of God, and His grace, is not always spread to people with gigantic revivals, or towering cathedrals. Sometimes people can accomplish much, much more, by doing good to one person at a time!

Thanks be to God!

Alan G. Vandewater
August 25, 2013

Luke 13: 10-17

10 Now he was teaching in one of the synagogues on the sabbath 11 And just then there appeared a woman with a spirit that had crippled her for eighteen years. She was bent over and was quite unable to stand up straight. 12 When Jesus saw her, he called her over and said "Woman, you are set free from your ailment." 13 When he laid his hands on her, immediately she stood up straight and began praising God. 14 But the leader of the synagogue, indignant because Jesus had cured on the sabbath, kept saying to the crowd, "There are six days on which work ought to be done; come on those days to be cured and not on the sabbath day."15 But the Lord answered him and said, "you hypocrites! Does not each of you on the sabbath untie his ox or his donkey from the manger and lead it to water?" 16 And ought not this woman, a daughter of Abraham whom Satan bound for eighteen long years, be set free from this bondage on the sabbath day?" 17 When he said this, all his opponents were put to shame; and the entire crowd was rejoicing at all the wonderful things he was doing.